Hobart Paperback No. 17

MARKETS UNDER THE SEA?

Markets under the Sea?

A study of the potential of private property rights in the seabed

D. R. Denman

*Professor Emeritus of Land Economy,
University of Cambridge*

with a Foreword by

JACK WISEMAN

*Professor of Economics,
University of York*

Published by
THE INSTITUTE OF ECONOMIC AFFAIRS
1984

First published in January 1984

© The Institute of Economic Affairs 1984

ISSN 0309-1783

ISBN 0-255 36168-8

Printed in Great Britain by
GORON PRO-PRINT CO LTD,
CHURCHILL INDUSTRIAL ESTATE, LANCING, WEST SUSSEX
Set in 'Monotype' Bembo

Contents

		Page
PREFACE	*Martin Wassell*	ix
FOREWORD	*Professor Jack Wiseman*	xii
THE AUTHOR		xvi

I. The Issues — 1
Subsidiary Questions — 2

II. What Resource? — 5
Land and Low Water — 5
The Land Analogy — 5
A market in rights — 6
'Seabed resource' — 7
Uses of the Seabed — 7
Familiar features — 8
Special features — 9
Charted Evidence — 11

III. Who Wants It? — 14
Where to Find Out — 14
(i) *National claims* — 15
Import dependence — 17
(ii) *Industrial and commercial activities* — 20
Sedentary fisheries — 20
Civil engineering — 22
Oil and mining companies — 23
Dredging companies — 24
Other activities — 25
(iii) *Thrust of technology* — 26
Transfer of technology — 27

IV. Who Holds It? 29

Zones and Jurisdictions 29
  Territorial sea 30
  Contiguous zone 31
  Continental shelf 31
  Continental margin 32
  Exclusive economic zone 32

The Common Heritage of Mankind 34
  Tenure to be challenged 36
  International monopoly 36
  A contradiction 38

Ownership and Property Rights 38
  'So with the seas, as with the land' 38
  Competence to create property 40
  Forms of ownership 41

V. Who Should Hold It? 45

Mine and Yours – to Enclose 45

Mine and Yours – to Choose 46
  Market choice – an example 48

Mine and Yours – to Exchange 49

Yes and No to the Seabed Monopolies 49
  Justifiable retention 51
  Wasting capital 51
  Losing rent 53
  Development inertia 54
  Monopoly charges 55

Uncommon Heritage 56

VI. What Chance an Open Market? 60

Opposing Fixed Ideas and Inertia 60
  Watching the national interest 62
  Pathways of reform 64

Getting Out of the Rut 65
  Costs of acquisition 66
  Brokerage costs 68

Benefits of experience   68
Planning control   69
Removing a basic confusion   69
Mutual Bonds of Freedom   71
   Give and take in the deep ocean   71
An Alternative International Arrangement   73
A Common Heritage to Private Property   73

VII. Conclusions   75

FURTHER READING   77

QUESTIONS FOR DISCUSSION   80

SUMMARY   *Back cover*

TABLES
  I. Non-fuel mineral imports as a percentage of national
     consumption in USA, 1979–82   18

  II. Non-fuel mineral imports as a percentage of national
     consumption of UK, EEC, Japan and W. Germany
     in 1977   18

  III. Developing countries' output of minerals also found
     in polymetallic nodules of the deep sea, 1980   19

  IV. Estimates of land-based reserves and nodule reserves
     of nickel, copper, cobalt and manganese   19

  V. Indices of past, present and future oil and gas activities
     on continental shelf of UK, USA, and Norway   21

FIGURES
  1. Continental Shelf UK: designated areas   33
  2. Continental shelf at fullest extent   35

Preface

Hobart Paperback 17 has been written by a leading authority on the analysis of property rights who, in the past 18 months or so, has established a reputation as one of the most incisive and persistent critics in Britain of the United Nations Convention on the Law of the Sea. That Convention opened for signature one year ago after almost a decade of some of the most intricate and complex international negotiations ever known. The United States having categorically refused to sign, the British Government announced that it would seek modifications before signing or ratifying the Convention (to date, 125 countries have signed and three have ratified). Professor Denman's critique would seem to suggest that the Government's decision was sound on both theoretical and practical grounds.

The eleven sessions of the Third UN Conference on the Law of the Sea (UNCLOS III) which hammered out the Convention were the result of two significant developments of modern times. The first was a trend among both developed and developing nations to seek to extend their territorial and economic claims over their coastal waters. The second was an advance in technology which has rendered feasible the exploitation of the mineral wealth and development potential of the seabed.

UNCLOS III arose out of a recognition by almost all nations that a new international legal régime would be desirable to govern the consequences of these two developments. The Convention as it now stands is thus about much more than the seabed. It purports to regularise within an agreed framework of international law other important matters such as freedom of navigation, the limits of territorial rights, exploitation of the economic resources of the continental shelf, the right of innocent passage, including that of warships and through international straits, pollution in the oceans, and fisheries. The provisions in the Convention for these matters have proved acceptable, and for the most part welcome, to the US and British Governments. What they have not been able to accept, and the reason for their

ix

refusal to sign, is the planned scheme for the exploitation of the seabed
of the deep ocean.

In pursuance of a UN resolution declaring the mineral wealth of
the ocean floor to be the 'common heritage of mankind', a majority
of nations – which included the land-locked and technologically
backward – sought to establish a collective international monopoly of
ownership and extraction of the resources on the deep-ocean seabed.
In contrast, those nations which possess the technical capability to
exploit the resources desired the maximum of international freedom
to do so. Both camps, however, recognised the need for an international treaty to establish an accepted legal framework within which
the exploitation of the seabed resources could proceed.

The scheme which was eventually adopted in the Convention
represents a compromise between the two camps. Unfortunately, as
Professor Denman explains, it is a collectivist, regulatory scheme with
redistributive purposes which, far from promoting investment in the
ocean seabed, would more likely have the effect of severely retarding
it – to the benefit of no nation on earth, whether rich or poor, technologically advanced or backward, land-locked or maritime. In brief,
the Convention provides for the establishment of an International
Seabed Authority (with a 36-member executive Council) in which
would be vested absolute and exclusive control over the seabed of
the deep oceans. The Authority would also possess an operational arm
– to be known as the Enterprise – which would itself engage in mining
and other commercial activities on behalf of the Authority and in competition with national state or private enterprises. Not only would
the Authority control access to the seabed; in order to obtain a
licence to mine a site, companies would have to identify and offer
the Enterprise a second prospected and matching site, *and* provide the
Enterprise with their expensively-developed technological know-
how to exploit it. The royalties and profits garnered by the Authority
would be distributed among member states, on some assessment of
'need'.

Professor Denman has no doubt that so highly-politicised a régime,
which gives scant consideration to both the value of intellectual
property and the high cost of prospecting two mining sites for every
one licensed, will hold back potential investors – whether private or
state enterprises – in their droves. His principal concern, however, is
the positive one of advancing proposals for an international legal

régime to govern the deep-ocean seabed which – in contrast to the paraphernalia of collectivist controls envisaged by the present Convention – will attract the maximum amount of investment to exploit the seabed's resources efficiently.

His starting point is that the state monopolies which, virtually by accident of history, have come to own and miscontrol the seabed beneath coastal waters must not, by extension, be the model for the establishment of a governmental *international* monopoly over the ocean seabed outside national jurisdictions. He examines at length the case for bringing the ownership and marketability of the seabed of national waters into closer conformity with the ownership and marketability of dry land. For market economies, this would mean denationalising the seabed and establishing private property rights. Professor Denman suggests how this might be done in Britain. His finishing point is a plea for individuals and companies to be accorded internationally-registrable titles, which would be absolute and marketable, in the seabed sites which they successfully explore and exploit through the application of their own capital and technical skills. This he sees as the most effective route to harnessing the wealth of the oceans which would, moreover, be compatible with benefitting mankind as a whole.

Professor Denman's *Hobart Paperback* is provocative and stimulating. As Professor Wiseman notes in his Foreword, it airs a number of fundamental issues about which there is much scope for further debate. Although the constitution of the Institute obliges it to dissociate its Trustees, Directors and Advisers from the author's analysis and conclusions, it offers this study as an informed and vigorous contribution to public discussion about an important subject which will remain a source of contention between nations for the foreseeable future whatever the fate of the present Convention.

December 1983   MARTIN WASSELL

Foreword

by Professor Jack Wiseman

I do not see the aim of my Foreword as being to offer either explanation or criticism of the details of this *Hobart Paperback*. Rather, I shall suggest to the reader the context within which it might be read. It is perhaps worth reiterating the purpose of the *Hobart Papers* and *Paperbacks*. It is not only to show how decentralised solutions (essentially, the use of markets) to economic problems are possible over a wider range of human situations than is commonly recognised, but also to suggest *operational* solutions to the particular problems discussed. Professor Denman's contribution qualifies on both counts but also goes beyond what is usual in that his preoccupation is not with new ways of economising existing resources but with the arrangements to economise a resource (the seabed) which has until recently been treated generally as a free good. There is thus the opportunity to influence outcomes at an earlier stage than usual. Time is nevertheless short, for attitudes are hardening and the pattern of property rights becoming circumscribed by the international character of negotiations over rights in the relevant assets, thereby embracing problems wider than those of property within a single jurisdiction. It is within this broader context that Professor Denman's operational proposals must be judged.

This said, I must confess that my reaction to an earlier version of this *Paper* was unenthusiastic; it seemed to me to beg too many questions for a (policy-oriented) *Hobart*. Simply, I was using an inappropriate standard. I should have appreciated that Professor Denman's contribution should be judged like the dog standing on its hind legs: the wonder is less that it should be done so well than that it should be done at all. This *Hobart Paperback* will leave unanswered questions in the mind of any intelligent reader. But that is unimportant beside the fact that he will be made to think about large questions whose significance may previously have escaped him.

Awareness of the importance in particular contexts of the absence of property rights in the seabed resource is not particularly new, though it has grown considerably in recent years with the opportunities for exploiting the seabed created by advancing technology. I myself first met the problem through an interest in fisheries economics. As economists began to trespass during the 1950s upon the territory formerly reserved for marine biologists, it was increasingly recognised that the central problem to be solved if markets were to function efficiently was the existence of common property (in other words, no property) in one of the factors of production – the relevant parts of the sea. While such recognition called into question the utility of 'solutions' which relied on various forms of regulation, however, this and other individual 'cases' were only slowly understood to be manifestations of a general problem. There were indeed economists who saw the need to develop a relevant law of the sea. Others, like me, saw the 'fishery case' (and similar ones) as a manifestation of a particular difficulty in the system of property rights rather than as a general problem of the importance it is now assuming.[1]

Professor Denman poses a series of cogent questions and, in seeking answers, advances a powerful argument for a 'market' solution to what might be called the 'micro-economics of seabed resource-allocation'. Workable and efficient micro-economic arrangements, however, depend here as elsewhere upon a clearly defined and accepted system of property rights and law concerned with the ownership of the particular resource. Professor Denman is fully aware of this condition. But because it seems to me to be the central problem to be solved, and because it raises so many and such difficult issues, my own concluding contribution is a restatement for the reader of some questions which this *Hobart Paperback* opens up for further debate.

1. The enclosure of the sea differs from earlier enclosure movements in the extent to which the resource lies outside individual national jurisdictions. The enclosure of the land in the UK, for example, took place generally within, or by simple extension of, an established body of law. Without doubt, it gave valuable rights to some

---

[1] It was common observation, of course, that individuals tried to create property rights at sea whenever possible, just as they do in other contexts. Deprived of legal sanctions, Maine fishermen, for example, have been said to be willing to enforce their 'entitlements' in their lobster pots with rifles.

citizens and denied them to others – but within a national jurisdiction.[2]

2. The precise form of enclosure will thus necessarily emerge from
negotiations between sovereign states. It is in this sense that we are
involved in an 'international redistribution of income' (or, more
properly, capital) *between sovereign states.*

3. The rights being negotiated supersede the 'entitlements' that individuals had previously established and exercised, for example, over
fishing grounds.[3]

4. It is not easy to see how this redistributive process can take place
other than by negotiations between sovereign states, hopefully
through the peaceful development of international law. Indeed, the
appropriate processes are already under way. The speculation that
a 'solution' might in time have emerged from individual behaviour
is of little practical importance. (Who would suggest that other
claims over 'property' have resulted from free transactions rather
than from coercion?)

5. It follows that the *form* taken by the law may determine the nature
of contractual relationships for generations to come. It is therefore
of primary importance that such matters as the *negotiability* of
property rights in the seabed be as simple (clearly transactable and
unambiguous) as humanly possible.

6. In a particular sense (Professor Denman treats this question much
more fully), the 'nationalisation' of the seabed is the natural outcome
of the international character of the problem. It is thus useful to
distinguish the *external* problem from the *internal* allocation of
rights. The latter may be thought of as one more problem of
privatisation, though a very special one. Further, the way in which
a private market in the 'UK seabed' could work would depend
upon the infrastructure of property rights created by other national
jurisdictions. How realistic is it to believe, however, that nations
with so wide a variety of political persuasions are going to participate in the creation of a common private market in the seabed?

---

[2] This is, of course, a description and not a justification.

[3] The virtual destruction of Hull as a deep-sea trawler port within a few years is a sufficient
illustration of the practical importance of this change.

7. Given that it is likely to be many years before such a solution could emerge, should not economists be seeking intellectual constructs better able to handle this kind of issue? The most promising possibility at the present time would seem to be the extension of the theory of public choice.

Let me reiterate in conclusion that the above observations are no more than a shopping list of some of my own reactions. The reader may find himself being provoked in quite different ways. In my eyes, that is the principal virtue of this *Hobart Paperback*.

University of York,   JACK WISEMAN
Institute of Social and Economic Research,
December 1983

The Author

DONALD DENMAN is Professor Emeritus of Land Economy in the University of Cambridge. He established the Department of Land Economy in 1962 and successfully launched the Land Economy Tripos at Cambridge some years later, covering land economy and agricultural and natural resource economics. His Cambridge initiative led to similar pioneering work in other universities in the Commonwealth and elsewhere; and to appointments as adviser and consultant to governments, international agencies and private concerns throughout the world.

Some six years ago, a research survey of the south Pacific, undertaken by Professor Denman for the Commonwealth Secretariat, brought home to him the future importance of the seabed resources and turned his attention to the ownership and management of them.

He has written, *inter alia*, 17 books in his specialised field, including: *Tenant Right Valuation in history and modern practice* (1942); *Estate Capital: The Contribution of Landownership to Agricultural Finance* (1957); *Origins of Ownership: A Brief History of Landownership and Tenure* (1958); *Farm Rents: a comparison of current and past farm rents in England and Wales* (1959); *Land in the Market* (IEA Hobart Paper No. 30, 1964); *Commons and Village Greens: a study in land use, conservation and management* (1967); *Rural Land Systems* (1968); *Land Use and the Constitution of Property* (1969); *Land Use: An Introduction to Proprietary Land Use Analysis* (1971); *The King's Vista: a land reform which has changed the face of Persia* (1973); *The Place of Property* (1978); *Land in a Free Society* (1980); *The Fountain Principle: A Guide to New Positive Rural Development Planning* (1982).

I. The Issues

If, in the words of Robbie Burns, the seas were to 'gang dry' and we could stand on the seabed as on dry land, the novelty would help us to appreciate, with a readier wit than we now possess, its place in the economic order of things. We would stand on an exposed continental shelf so broad as to multiply the land mass of Britain by a factor of three. More startling still would be the realisation that every step we took was on Crown land and that, therefore, over 60 per cent of the nation's physical resources are state property and in a sense national-ised. And what is true for Britain is true for every other country with sea coasts and maritime approaches – including the USA, the pride of free markets and of private property. Furthermore, beyond the jurisdiction of specific nations lies the seabed of the deep oceans. Even there, according to the provisions of the recently-signed Law of the Sea Convention, it is proposed to vest the resource absolutely in an inter-national corporation, the International Seabed Authority (ISA), to be administered as 'the common heritage of mankind'.

The seabed is, relatively, a virgin realm. Until recently, it had been virtually a no-man's land. With few exceptions, no-one had bothered to lay claim to it. That attitude, however, has now become old-fashioned. It has given way to an intent to apprehend and appropriate; for modern technology has brought the seabed resource within the range of profitable exploitation. Although industry has been the pioneer of the newly-applied sciences and technology, governments have provided the vanguard of diplomacy necessary to establish national spheres of operation. Inevitably, therefore, the state has been the frontiersman, staking out national claims. In thus establishing their sovereignties, governments have almost inadvertently assumed property rights, or something like them, over the seabed. The fact of state ownership raises the question of its continuation and its role in the seabed economies of the future. It is the purpose of this *Hobart Paperback* to take up that question.

For the supreme title to all or most of the seabed to vest in the state

1

could have serious economic and social consequences – if not now, then most certainly later. What, and how serious, those consequences might be will depend upon the purposes for which the state holds the title, and also upon the extent to which there is a demand for private ownership of the resource. When new territory was opened up in places like America and Australia, the state played a critical role in allocating the virgin public lands to private ownership,[1] a benign and constructive function in a nascent economy. The frontiers of today and tomorrow lie in the seabed and the state may have a similar constructive role to play. Even so, if no-one wants the wilderness or the seabed, it does not matter whether they are held in public or private hands.

If the purpose of the state title is to subordinate the proprietorship and use of the seabed to the arbitrary and permanent authority of the state, the distribution of the resource to meet manifest demands for it is likely to be inefficient, and the liberties that reside in private property will be curtailed. To the extent that this is true of a national state, it is even more so when the supreme authority is international.

When, therefore, we inquire about the role of the state in the seabed economies of tomorrow, we are raising issues about the nature of the seabed resource itself, the demand for it, and whether the present state titles should be temporary expedients or permanent institutions.

Subsidiary Questions

This *Hobart Paperback* attempts to provide an answer by examining five subsidiary questions: What is the seabed resource? Who wants it? Who holds it? Who should have it? and What chance is there of an open market to handle its distribution?

Section II responds to the first question by explaining the divide between land and sea and, on the view that the seabed is the continuation under the sea of the land mass, postulates a market for the seabed resource analogous to a market for land. A distinction is drawn between a market for the seabed as a resource in itself and markets for its several components. A broad classification is made of these components into those which bear similarity to features of the

---

[1] A large proportion of the Public Lands of the USA are still unallocated and recent studies have made a case for speeding up distribution into private hands. (John Baden, *Earth Day Reconsidered*, The Heritage Foundation, Washington DC, 1980.)

land mass and others which are special to the sea. The picture thus drawn is rounded off by a brief comment on the progress made to date in surveying and charting the seas and the seabed.

Section III examines first of all the evidence on which judgements can be made of the present and likely future demands for access to and ownership of the seabed resource. National demands as manifested in actual ownership and sovereignty rights are examined and the tangible benefits of acquisition are touched upon from a national viewpoint. Industrial and commercial attitudes and the demands which derive from them are then assessed, albeit from an inevitably speculative angle. Finally, the all-important thrust of advances in technology upon past, present and future demands is given its due attention.

Section IV focusses attention on the supply side of a market for the seabed resource. Convention and tradition have apportioned the seabed and seas into zones of sovereign rights and jurisdictions. These, as areas over which the recipient states have powers of disposal, are defined. Beyond the national jurisdictions, the Law of the Sea Convention proposes to set up the International Seabed Authority. Its unprecedented monopolistic potential is recognised as a powerhouse to be reckoned with among the sovereignties of the world's seabed. Property rights and not sovereignty, however, determine and justify a resource market. The relationship between them is therefore examined and the run of public and private property rights over the seabed is illustrated by selected examples.

Section V considers how a market for the seabed resource might be constituted and function. It examines, first, the enclosure of resources by the bounds of property rights – the divide of mine from yours; secondly, the benefits of a fully-functioning market, the freedom to choose and exchange; and, thirdly, the reality of the seabed monopolies and the arguments for supporting or rejecting them. The final paragraph explains an inescapable contradiction which will confront the International Seabed Authority as the agent for the common heritage of mankind.

Section VI looks to the future and provides a brief analysis of the attitudes, doctrine and habits characteristic of the present owners of the seabed and of those who support the *status quo*. Consideration is given to the extent to which those attitudes and conditions are obstacles to the creation of a market for the seabed resource. To balance this approach from the supply side, the reaction of those who could become buyers and traders in a market for the seabed resource is weighed as a critical factor which could influence change.

Finally, we return to the contradiction inherent in the proposed world administration for the seabed of the deep oceans and contemplate various alternatives, some of which have already been acted upon while others are still in the womb of tentative suggestion.

II. What Resource?

Land and Low Water

The seabed is a physical continuation of the land-mass under the sea[1] and any definition of it must locate the divide between land and sea. Nature is no help. At low tide the sea estuaries of lowland rivers are expanses of mud flats; and where fens run to the coast the sea is often an horizon of silver over wide sands. Do we conclude, then, that land and sea have no fixed boundary?

Where nature is uncertain, the law comes to our aid. Numerous countries, including the UK, have decreed that, as a general rule, the seas proper shall start at low-water mark.[2] There are exceptions, however. Bluff cliffs, coasts with deeply-indented bays, inlets and fiords, and the scattered islands of archipelagos require the divide to be arbitrarily drawn as a web of 'base lines' spun across the mouths of bays and from headland to headland.[3] Where this happens, the expanse of waters in an estuary or bay is divided between the 'seas' proper and the waters on the landward side of the division, the 'inland' and 'internal waters'. Often, as in the UK, Crown or state ownership of the seabed of the territorial seas is coterminous with a like ownership of the beds of tidal inland and internal waters. We must take care, however, not to be too pedantic about the legal definition of the 'seas' and the seabed lest we lose sight of the Crown or state monopoly that lies in the seabed beneath the landward waters. In this *Hobart Paperback*, therefore, the term 'seabed resource' is used liberally and makes no distinction between the seabed of the 'seas' and that of the tidal inland and internal waters.

The Land Analogy

That the seabed resource in physical form is a continuation of the land-

---

[1] Cf. the Truman Proclamation of 1945 which states that 'the continental shelf may be regarded as an extension of the land-mass of the coastal nation . . .'.

[2] Low-water mark is variously defined but is normally taken as meaning between Spring and neap tides.

[3] Below, p. 30.

mass under the sea[4] and, by that criterion, analogous to it forms the basis of our main contention that the creation of a market in the seabed resource similar to a market in land is a proposal worthy of consideration. Let us, therefore, briefly examine the function of the market in land and pursue the parallel from there.

A market in rights

When a transaction is made in the land market, the purchased possession cannot be handed over from seller to buyer like a packet of cigarettes over the counter. In a primitive society, the buyer would come to the land itself and a sod of earth or some other symbol would be exchanged to signify the vesting of possession in the new landholder. In the language of the old lawyers, 'seisin' (possession) would be delivered to the new hands. Where the law is more advanced, the purchaser takes possession under the authority of a 'deed of grant' confirming to the world that title to the land has passed to him. Ownership 'lies in grant' and not in the action of overt delivery. The deed of grant conveys a right of some kind. The nature of the right will depend upon the juridical system governing the transaction. Under the legal codes of Europe, the highest right is a right to property in the land itself; under the common law of England, it is at most a right to an 'estate' or interest in the land granting power to possess, use and dispose. Estates differ according to the character and duration of the property rights which constitute them. Lesser rights abound in various forms to make up the merchandise of the land market: rights, for example, to use the land only for passage or for pasture, and rights to the benefits of restrictive covenants over neighbouring land. In short, a land market deals in property rights rather than in the land itself.

There are today property rights in the seabed which have all the makings of the merchandise of a resource market similar to a market in land. The full extent and nature of the seabed rights, however, differ within the zones and sovereignties that divide the seas.[5] The picture is confusing at present. The seabed of a nation's territorial sea is normally subject to property rights which give full ownership in

---

[4] In the USA the seabed resources of the Outer Continental Shelf are administered by the Bureau of Lands of the Department of the Interior which was set up to administer the Public Lands.

[5] Below, pp. 29-34.

the conventional sense.[6] Further out, in the continental shelf, sovereign rights of exploitation as recognised under the UN Law of the Sea Convention of 1958 are usually established by the municipal law of the coastal state. Although these rights are used by governments to grant licences and leases to private concerns – that is, to grant rights similar to property rights – it is debatable whether, at present, the seabeds of the continental shelves are formally owned. Indeed, in the interests of the development of a resource market, it is one of the purposes of this *Hobart Paperback* to ask how long it will be before strict legal form removes this uncertainty.

'Seabed resource'

For a full understanding of the land market, we must also know what is meant by the word 'land' itself. To the economist, 'land' is one of the three factors of production and, unlike 'capital', has a usefulness which owes nothing to human labour.[7] It is the soil and its subsoil in the original state of nature. To the lawyer, however – and, for that matter, to the layman of common speech – 'land' includes the surface of the earth and all the things of a physical nature above or below it, adjacent and attached to it, such as buildings and their fixtures, trees and minerals.[8] In considering the seabed as a resource and the market or potential market in it, we shall use the term 'seabed resource' in the same comprehensive, pragmatic way that the lawyer speaks of land.

Uses of the Seabed

The subject of this *Paperback* is the prospect for an open market in the seabed as a resource in itself. We are not directly concerned with markets for the specific elements of which the seabed resource as a whole is composed – minerals, petroleum, shellfish and the like. Admittedly, markets for each of these elements will be immediately affected by the manner in which the seabed resource as a whole is held and marketed. Indeed, an important aspect of our analysis will

---

[6] There are exceptions; the territory of the realm of Belgium, for example, extends only to low-water mark and does not reach to the seabed of the territorial sea.

[7] Alfred Marshall, *Principles of Economics*, Macmillan, London, 1964 edn., p. 120.

[8] G. C. Cheshire, *The Modern Law of Real Property*, Butterworth & Co., 5th edn., London, 1944, p. 100.

be the relationship between the market for the seabed resource and the markets for each of its components. If the Crown, for example, has an absolute right of ownership over the seabed resource of the territorial seas, this monopoly will affect transactions in the minerals extracted from the seabed.

Having drawn so close an analogy between land and the seabed resource, we must now acknowledge a fundamental difference: that the seabed resource is, for the most part, approachable only through superjacent waters. This obstacle is the reason why the seabed was not appropriated by private hands long ago. Now that technology is making the seabed accessible through the waters, the means of so doing are critical to the marketing of the seabed.

Demand in a land market derives from many sources, but always in response to a desire to use the potentialities of the land for one purpose or another. Thus, if we are to judge the prospects for a market in the seabed resource, we must have some idea of what the market has, or might have, to offer – that is to say, of the uses of the seabed resource. To complete the picture, it would help to know what progress is being made towards a cartographical record of the seabed. The following paragraphs attempt to fill those gaps, although space permits only the broadest of generalisations.

Familiar features

Because the seabed resource is a continuation of the land-mass, it has many attributes which are similar to the familiar features of dry land. It also has its own special attributes. We will briefly consider both.

With so much limelight turned on dramatic discoveries like oil and nodules, we are apt to overlook the simple truth that the seabed (which extends over some 362 million square kilometres[9]) provides a foundation – a bedrock for whoever wishes to build upon it, lay installations on its surface, and anchor craft and floating devices in it. This physical function of the seabed will become more and more important as the design and creation of artificial islands for many different purposes gathers momentum throughout the world.[10]

---

[9] A. A. Archer, 'Deep Sea Mining: A Survey of Manganese Nodule Resources', Society for Underwater Technology Conference, London, 30 June 1982.

[10] John E. Allen, 'Artificial Islands: hope for a congested landscape', *Journal of British Aerospace Aircraft Group*, February 1982.

Petroleum, natural gas, coal and the aggregates of sand and gravel are commodities which in or on the seabed resemble their counterparts on dry land. The techniques of extracting oil, gas and coal from the seabed do not differ fundamentally from those used on land. An oil-well is an oil-well wherever it is, even if wells in the sea with their rigs and platforms are relatively more costly to drill and service. A coal-face deep in the subsoil of the seabed can differ little from a coal-face anywhere; in the future, the former may well be ventilated and served by shafts driven through artificial islands built up from the seabed to the surface.[11] As with coal, other mineral-bearing strata run out from the land into the seabed, sometimes to outcrop there as 'lodes'; formal explorations and accidental finds, as with the magnetite deposit off St. David's Head,[12] are continually adding to knowledge. The aggregates of sand and gravel on the seabed do not differ from those on land, although to dredge them at sea is a more capital-intensive enterprise than quarrying them on land.

Special features

The seabed resource and the associated seas also have characteristics peculiar to themselves which are either intrinsically different from anything found on land or which take special forms fashioned by the maritime environment.

Fish stocks are the most important of the sea's biological resources. Species differ in their relationship to the seabed. The shellfish (crustaceans and molluscs) live on or in the rocks, sands and muds; demersal fish (cod, plaice and their like) live and feed on or near the sea bottom; and a third type, the pelagic species (mackerel, pilchard and others), moves in shoals in the waters between the surface and the bottom. Their relationship to the seabed is crucial to the owning and running of exclusive fisheries for breeding, rearing and harvesting fish, either on the seabed or in the waters.

Seaweeds promise to play a useful part in the future economy of the oceans. Kelp has long been harvested from the seabed and shores. Today science can convert the vegetation into foods for man and beast and into fertilisers and fibres, and can even use it in the synthetic

---

[11] B. E. W. Dowse, 'The Role of Hybrid Islands for Offshore Coal Mining', Oceanology International Conference, Brighton, 1980.

[12] *House of Lords Official Report (Hansard)*, 19 January 1981, para. 265.

production of methane and gasoline. Experiments are pointing the way to aquaculture enterprises running kelp farms over extensive areas of the sub-littoral waters of the world.[13] Other forms of aquaculture are being developed to farm the seas and seabed.

Just as aquaculture depends upon the use of nitrates and phosphates drawn up from the deeper waters of the ocean, so the warm upper layers of tropical seas are being tapped by means of ocean thermal energy conservation (OTEC). This new technology has recently received special legislative backing in the USA[14] and, if it advances, could spawn platforms and submersibles occupying exclusive areas.

Mineral resources peculiar to the seas and seabed are found in suspension in the sea water – notably salt and magnesium; in polymetallic sulphide muds; in diamond-bearing gravels and silicon-bearing sands; in what are called 'placers'[15] (that is, loose detrital matter dispersed from mineral outcrops); and in manganese and phosphorite nodules on the ocean floor. The sulphide muds, the latest discovery in the inventory of seabed minerals, are being pumped to the surface from specially-designed vessels. The diamond lift is a local speciality of Namibia. And silicon usage is little more than a scientist's hypothesis.

Attention is at present focussed on manganese nodules. Peculiar to the deep oceans, manganese or polymetallic nodules lie like great pebbles on the ocean floor at depths of 5,000 metres and over. As the intensity of international political interest in them testifies, they are reckoned as a future source of considerable wealth as soon as they are within range of economic exploitation. Estimates of their abundance and intrinsic worth, however, are highly speculative. Not only is it extremely difficult to sample the deposits where they lie; to measure their economic significance requires evidence of the minerals which compose the nodules and of the efficiency of the techniques for mining them. Reliable figures[16] indicate that, given the capabilities of the 'first generation' of mining and processing equipment now in

[13] H. A. Wilcox, 'Ocean Farming: Prospects and Problems', *Span* (international journal of the Royal Dutch/Shell Group) Vol. 23, No. 2, 1980.

[14] *Ocean Thermal Energy: Prospects and Opportunities,* Policy Research in Engineering, Science and Technology (*Prest*), University of Manchester, July 1981.

[15] D. S. Cronan, 'Geochemical Exploration for Shallow Water Mineral Deposits', Oceanology International Conference, Brighton, 1980.

[16] A. A. Archer, 'Manganese nodules as a source of nickel, copper, cobalt and manganese', Institution of Mining and Metallurgy, *Transactions*, Section A, Vol. 90, January 1981.

prospect, it will be essential for the nickel and copper content of the nodules to average at least 2·25 per cent to make mining economical. And there are other tests and markers. For example, where the amount of nodules in bulk is less than 5 kilograms per square metre, the site is probably best avoided.

The sum of the current evidence points to a 15 per cent coverage of the deep ocean beds by manganese nodules, totalling some 550 billion (wet) tonnes. After applying the economic tests mentioned above, and allowing for wastage and mining inefficiencies, the figure falls to between 15 and 25 billion (wet) tonnes, with the preponderance in the Pacific Ocean and the lowest supplies in the Atlantic. It has been calculated that the present economically recoverable resources of the deep oceans could potentially contribute to the world supply of minerals in the following magnitudes:

		million tonnes
Nickel	–	25–40
Copper	–	20–30
Cobalt	–	3–5
Manganese	–	500–800

Raw sea water *per se* is used as the sole input in the desalination process which usually takes place in land-based plants; and the new techniques invented to harness the energy in the movements of waves and tides operate with the sea water alone. Added to this, the seas and the seabed have become ever-open dumping grounds for wastage from industrial and urban shores. Such uses lay claims upon the seas and seabed which could not be ignored by the owners of the seabed resource. Finally, the ecologists are demanding areas to be set aside as maritime nature reserves.[17]

Charted Evidence

The owners of the seabed resource will, if they are to develop a market in it, require maps and charts of the seabed to record its boundaries, its morphology, the pattern of its uses and the whereabouts of its physical components. Much has yet to be done, especially in mapping boundaries and proprietary interests, to demonstrate what might be

---

[17] *The Conservation and Development Programme for the UK; a response to the World Conservation Strategy*, Kogan Page, London, 1983.

in the shop-window of a seabed resource market. The present close co-operation between hydrographers and scientists holds out considerable promise. Of particular interest is the work of the International Hydrographic Organisation (IHO) at Monaco. This pioneer in international co-operation for the better understanding of the oceans has recently completed a series of small-scale[18] charts covering the world's oceans; and other work is in hand to provide regional charts of a similar nature but on a larger scale.[19] In addition to these nautical charts, the IHO, in conjunction with the Intergovernmental Oceanographic Commission (IOC) of UNESCO and other international scientific bodies, has brought up to date the General Bathymetric Chart of the Oceans (GEBCO). Besides the contours of the seabed, the modern version provides scientific data by world-renowned marine geologists and geophysicists.

At present, the IHO has 50 member-states. Each of these 'charting nations' operates a hydrographic service, although the levels of technical achievement vary widely.[20] Prominent among them are the UK and USA which offer a world-wide service, a facility of special value to the non-charting countries of the developing world. National and regional charts have been much enriched in recent years to show new aspects of the seas and the seabed, morphological features, zonal boundaries, fishery limits, sedimentary basins, other geological phenomena, and the proprietary structure of leases and licences for energy resources. Recent studies have provided cartographical information on particular features of the seabed, notably the location of polymetallic nodule deposits recorded by the Scripps Institution of Oceanography, Sediment Data Bank.

It is universal practice at present for promoters and operators to make their own detailed surveys of possible hydrocarbon deposits and mineral sites and to map these for incorporation in national records and charts.[21] A similar practice is followed where civil engineers use the seabed for the foundations of structures or for dredging. Not all nations can serve themselves in this manner. Of the 131 maritime members of the United Nations, only 50 or so are chart-

---

[18] 1:10,000,000 and 1:3,500,000.

[19] 1:1,000,000.

[20] Full details of each nation's service are given in a Yearbook published by the IHO.

[21] In some countries, notably Norway, government surveys contribute basic data in considerable detail and extent.

makers; others have hydrographic departments of government, and the rest have no facilities at all.[22] One of the objectives of the IHO is to help the ill-equipped nations by arranging for competent countries to sponsor chart-making programmes for them.

In organising introductions in this way, the IHO has established a model which could be followed to practical advantage in other seabed development operations. A nation which has embarked upon a marine resource development policy the first step of which requires the charting of its seas and seabed is introduced to another nation which will co-operate with it in a spirit that respects the dignity of both parties. Each strikes its own bargain in its own way and neither loses its identity in collective anonymity. Every help should therefore be given to strengthen, financially and otherwise, the work of the IHO. Detailed charting by individual nations of the maritime zones will be more essential than ever if national seabed resources are to be identified and catalogued for the market.

---

[22] Rear-Admiral G. S. Ritchie, 'The New Challenge Facing the World's Hydrographers', F.I.G. XVI International Congress, Montreux, Switzerland, 1981.

III. Who Wants It?

Where to Find Out
This Section examines the demand side of a market for the seabed resource and asks who might want to buy or own the seabed.

The present ownership pattern of the seabed resource is itself a form of evidence. Within the confines of allocation procedures, demand has been satisfied to some degree. The present owners would presumably not take or hold possession of resources they did not want. Unfortunately, the current state of affairs is everywhere dominated by the near-absolute ownership, or its equivalent, vested in national governments. Universal state ownership of the supreme title gives the state paramount control over the supply of property rights in the seabed resource. So imperial a control creates a monopoly which comes very near to being absolute. By their very existence, the state monopolies block the growth of market exchange transactions in absolute property rights; and, by restricting the right of alienation, they indirectly control the pattern of transactions in those lesser rights which are derived from the absolute supreme titles. Interference in the market in this way blurs the evidence which could otherwise point to potential demand. Furthermore, we would be able to judge more accurately what the future demands for absolute property rights in the seabed resource might be if we knew the reasons why the present monopolistic owners wished to retain their titles. This aspect of the demand side of the market is governed to a large extent by who holds the resource and, hence, is better left to Section IV.

We can make some headway here by conjecturing how those who now have lesser, derivative rights in the seabed resource (lessees, licensees) would react to opportunities to acquire absolute rights of ownership or their equivalent over the seabed resource. A readiness to respond could be interpreted as a signal that an open market in property rights would stimulate a demand not only from the present holders of the lesser rights but also from others who have hitherto shown no interest in the seabed resource because they were unwilling to hold derivative rights.

14

Like the demand for property rights in land, that for property rights in the seabed resource is motivated by a desire to obtain the power to use the resource for one purpose or another. The mineral lease is entered into, not for its own sake as a property right, but to get at the minerals. Section II described the uses made of the seabed resource. Our quest for evidence about what the demand schedule might be in a market for the seabed resource must try to identify the nature and sources of the present and future demands for these uses, irrespective of the form of property rights in the seabed resource itself. We can proceed in three ways, by examining: (i) national claims to the seabed; (ii) commercial and industrial exploitation of it; and (iii) how innovations, new ideas and advanced technology make access to the seabed possible.

(i) *National claims*

In adjudicating disputes in 1964 and 1965 between Germany, the Netherlands and Denmark on the boundaries of their respective continental shelves, the International Court of Justice 'entertained'

'what is no doubt the most fundamental of all the rules of law relating to the continental shelf, enshrined in Article 2 of the 1958 Geneva Convention, though quite independent of it – namely that the rights of the coastal State in respect of the area of the continental shelf that constitutes a natural prolongation of its land territory into and under the sea exist *ipso facto* and *ab initio*, by virtue of its sovereignty over the land and as an extension of it in an exercise of sovereign rights for the purpose of exploring the seabed and exploiting its natural resources'.[1]

This dictum has an historical significance. It established that it was not the 1958 Convention on the Continental Shelf and similar international treaties *per se* which started the post-1945 scramble among the nations to claim exclusive sovereignty over the seabed resource adjacent to their coasts. The treaties merely gave formal expression to the awakening realisation that the exigencies of the modern world economy had made the seas and the seabed a realm of scarce resources, whereas our forefathers had always assumed that nature was in limitless abundance there.

International law had long recognised a nation's full sovereignty over its territorial waters, but more for purposes of navigational control

---

[1] *North Sea Continental Shelf Cases (1969)*, ICJ Rep. (1969) 3, 53.

and juridical authority than for economic exploitation. The economic pressures which have stimulated the creation of continental shelves, exclusive economic zones and other divisions of the seabed and seas (Section IV) have increased the economic importance of the resources of the territorial waters. The one-time economic no-man's-land of the seabed has, in its coastal areas, been partitioned among the nations into exclusive sovereignties for exploiting its resources. Sovereignty, whether limited (as in Article 2(1) of the 1958 Convention on the Continental Shelf) to exploring and exploiting natural resources, or full-ranged, has in its gift powers akin to ownership. The British Continental Shelf Act of 1964 makes no formal reference to ownership of Britain's continental shelf but specifically extends the ownership of petroleum in the land, which was vested in the state in 1934, to the seabed. The designation of continental shelves, the widening of territorial waters, and the premature establishment of exclusive economic zones have clearly demonstrated the demands of maritime countries for true or quasi-ownership of the seabed resource under their coastal waters. The move to set up an International Seabed Authority (ISA) for the deep oceans is no more than a grand endorsement of the more or less world-wide nationalistic demands for some stake in the seabed resource. Thus, individually or collectively, national demands for rights over the seabed resource have been expressed. There is no evidence to suggest that these demands, strengthened rather than weakened by time and scarcity, will not continue into the future.

When the Convention on the Continental Shelf was signed in 1958, very little was known for certain about the bounty in the seabed of coastal waters and no-one took the deep oceans seriously in this respect. Drilling for oil and gas began in US Federal waters in 1954; and the first exploration licences for the Norwegian continental shelf were granted in 1963. Britain's first offshore gas find came in 1964 and oil was no more than an exciting hope until 1969. Nevertheless, 46 nations signed the Convention; national hopes are better secured than let slip. Financially, only a cockleshell of cost was involved to pass legislation ratifying the Convention, for security of the sovereign rights carried no obligation to commit capital to the exploitation of the seabed.[2] Now and for the future, the scene is less hazy. Much more

---

[2] *Convention on the Continental Shelf (1958)*, Article 2(3).

is known of what the seabed has to offer in the deep and in the shallow. It is the cost that causes apprehension. At present, for example, oil-generated energy is no more than 26 per cent of the cost of tapping the kinetic energy of the waves;[3] and Professors Sorenson and Mead some years ago published cautionary cost-benefit studies of mining deep-sea nodules.[4]

Import dependence

The advantage of securing *national* supplies of primary resources will keep up the pressure for nations to ring-fence their coastal zones and, in addition, to claim proprietary rights in the deep ocean bed.[5] National demands for the use of the seabed resource are not so novel that they cannot be illustrated from past and current practice. The following paragraphs and Tables give specific examples of national wants being met wholly or in part from the seabed resource.

The major industrial nations, singly or in groups, generate the bulk of world demand for minerals, metallic and otherwise. In some instances, home production is sufficient to satisfy consumption, with or without the help of the seabed – as, for example, with Canada's nickel output. The majority of the industrial nations with market economies, however, are not self-sufficient. They depend on imports, sometimes heavily so, and especially for the four metals (copper, cobalt, nickel and manganese) found in the seabed resource of the deep oceans. Tables I and II illustrate this point.

It is the developing countries which, in large measure, supply the world's exports, notably of the 'seabed minerals' (Table III). The neat balance of supply and demand is likely, perhaps, to be severely disturbed by mining the deep seabed. Crude calculations have been made of the land-based reserves of the four minerals and of the probable contribution to supply of the seabed nodules (Table IV). Providing the economics and conditions of access are right, the Tables indicate clearly the advantage to the industrial countries of mining the deep

---

[3] W. Schmitt, 'Ocean Energy on Parade', in *More than Enough?*, The Unesco Press, 1982, p. 85.

[4] P. E. Sorenson and W. J. Mead, 'A Cost Benefit Analysis of Ocean Mineral Resource Development: the Case of Manganese Nodules', *American Journal of Agricultural Economics*, 1968, pp. 1,611-1,620.

[5] When the Third Law of the Sea Conference adopted the Convention on the Law of the Sea on 30 April 1982, 130 nations voted in favour out of a total of 151.

TABLE I

NON-FUEL MINERAL IMPORTS AS A PERCENTAGE
OF NATIONAL CONSUMPTION IN USA, 1979-82

Mineral	1979 %	1980 %	1981 %	1982* %
Cobalt	94	93	91	100
Copper	12	14	5	43
Gold	50	18	7	68
Manganese	98	98	98	100
Nickel	69	73	72	93
Sand and Gravel	E	E	E	E
Silver	42	7	50	72
Iron Core	25	25	28	28
Tin	80	79	80	90
Vanadium	28	17	42	42

*Estimated.

E=net exports.

Sources: *Mineral Commodity Summaries 1982*, Department of the Interior, Bureau of Mines, Washington DC.

TABLE II

NON-FUEL MINERAL IMPORTS AS A PERCENTAGE OF NATIONAL
CONSUMPTION OF UK, EEC, JAPAN AND W. GERMANY IN 1977

Country	Cobalt %	Copper %	Manganese %	Nickel %	Iron %	Tin %
UK	100	82	100	100	89	65
EEC	100	81	100	100	79	87
Japan	n.a.	90	90	100	94	97
W. Germany	n.a.	100	n.a.	n.a.	93	n.a.

Source: P. Crowson, *Non-Fuel Minerals and Foreign Policy*, Royal Institute for International Affairs, 8 July 1977; and Yuan-li Wu, *Raw Material Supply in a Multipolar World*, National Strategy Information Center Inc., New York.

seabed. It could reduce demand from the industrial countries for land-based supplies and, in consequence, reduce prices.

The continental shelves of the industrial nations, with their supplies of oil and gas, have attracted the most interest and activity over the last 20 years or so. Their known commercially exploitable reserves and estimates of their recoverable resources point to profitable oppor-

TABLE III

DEVELOPING COUNTRIES' OUTPUT OF MINERALS ALSO
FOUND IN POLYMETALLIC NODULES OF THE DEEP SEA, 1980*

Country	Nickel %A	%B	Copper %A	%B	Cobalt %A	%B	Manganese %A	%B
Chile			13·3	45·7				
Papua/ New Guinea			2·0	41·4				
Peru			4·6	19·4				
Philippines	10·1	4·9	3·7	9·4	5·0	1·1		
Zaire			5·7	43·2	51·0	21·1		
Zambia			7·3	88·7	9·2	6·9		
Cuba	5·5	5·1						
Botswana	0·8	21·0						
Gabon							6·2	9·5
Brazil	3·0						7·9	1·0
India							6·2	1·0
New Caledonia	21·0							
Indonesia	13·7	1·0						
Zimbabwe	0·9	5·9						
	55·0		36·6		65·2		20·3	

*In some cases 1978 or 1979.

%A= percentage of world supply.
%B= percentage of total national export revenue.

Source: Third UN Law of Sea Conference publication A/CONF. 62/L.84, 2 March 1982

TABLE IV

ESTIMATES OF LAND-BASED RESERVES AND NODULE RESERVES
OF NICKEL, COPPER, COBALT AND MANGANESE

(million tonnes metal content)

Mineral	Land-based	Estimated nodule potential
Nickel	60	290
Copper	505	240
Cobalt	3·4	60
Manganese	5,400	6,000

Sources: UN Department of International Economic and Social Affairs, publication
ST/ESA/107, 1980; and Mineral Commodity Summaries 1982, Bureau of Mines,
Department of the Interior, Washington DC.

tunities for those who now hold sovereignty over them. Table V indicates past and present performance and future potentialities for the UK, USA and Norway.

(ii) *Industrial and commercial activities*

In the current days of the seabed era, industrial and commercial enterprise is already represented by a wide variety of operators, from the major national oil companies to the one-man shellfish farmers. Every concern, however, both large and small, needs a property right in the seabed. The spate of investment and development activity suggests that today's demands are the vanguard of tomorrow's ever-multiplying claims.

Our concern here is with the differing commercial and industrial activities which use the seabed and, in consequence, require property rights in it. Ultimately, we want to use this evidence to help us judge what the future demands from commerce and industry for the ownership and marketing of the seabed resource might be. It was stated earlier that we cannot with confidence ascertain the demands for fuller property rights of the present holders of licences and leases in the seabed. We are ignorant because they are given no opportunities to express their demands through an open market. There are, however, certain significant pointers.

Sedentary fisheries

Among the humbler activities on the seabed are fisheries in what the UN Law of the Sea Convention calls 'sedentary fish',[6] that is, fish which live in, on or near the seabed (in the main, all manner of shellfish).

Shellfish, and particularly oysters, are either gathered naturally or 'farmed'. Ideally, fisheries should enjoy exclusive rights. In countries like Britain, there have existed for generations areas of the seabed which are privately owned as shellfish fisheries, but the examples are far too few to have had any effect on the power of the Crown monopoly. Demand for exclusive rights is unsatisfied, so much so that legislation has been passed empowering the government to create private,

---

[6] Article 77 (4).

TABLE V

INDICES OF PAST, PRESENT AND FUTURE OIL AND GAS ACTIVITIES ON CONTINENTAL SHELF OF UNITED KINGDOM, UNITED STATES AND NORWAY

Activity	UK	USA	Norway
Wells drilled: (dates)	(1972–81) 1,458	(1956–81) 19,744[1]	(1966–81) 311
Output: (1981)			
Oil	89·4 omt	286 mb	23·5 omt
Gas	32·1 omt	4·88 tcf	25·2 omt
Reserves:			
proven, probable:			
Oil	2,300 mt	3·8 bb	} 2,700 omt
Gas	1,405 bcm	13·0 tcf	
recoverable:			
Oil	2,100–4,300 mt	43·5 bb	} 4,200–5,000 omt
Gas	1,350–2,250 bcm	230·6 tcf	

Symbols: omt=oil equivalent million tons   mb=million barrels
mt =million tonnes   bb =billion barrels
bcm=billion cubic metres   tcf =trillion cubic feet.

[1] Federal waters only; 8,000 more in State waters.

Sources: Annual Report 1981, Oljedirektoratet, Oslo, Norway; Department of the Interior, Minerals Management Service, *Fact Sheet,* 2 September 1982, Washington DC; *Brown Book 1982,* Department of Energy, London.

exclusive fisheries in severalty.[7] The demands for such rights, and the tenacity with which present owners hold on to their seabed interests, are reliable indicators of what the response to full ownership over the seabed resource might be from the operators of sedentary and other fisheries. An example was where an oyster farmer readily took a long lease of the entire seabed of an estuarine river when it was offered to him by the owners who had acquired it from the Crown.[8]

The scene in America is far more active. In state waters off the east coast, submerged lands (so-called 'barren bottoms') have long been held on 20-year leases for the creation of private, exclusive oyster beds. The Maryland seabed lessees have full property rights under its landlord and tenant laws.[9] The supply of leases is controlled by the State with its superior title to the seabed; in 1979, 9,000 acres were leased in Maryland waters, leaving a further 50,000 acres to meet a vigorous and growing demand.

The celebrated shellfish grounds along the Atlantic littoral of France are the scene today of a pitched battle between the families of the traditional fishermen and commercial interests. Long practice has wrought the conviction that the licences to farm and take oysters and shellfish granted by the local government are inheritable and exclusive to the family; commercial firms oppose the notion and are demanding similar facilities for themselves and other corporate bodies.

Civil engineering

In the more substantial realm of civil engineering – leaving to one side for the moment oil, gas and mineral extraction – there is an ever-increasing demand for property rights over the seabed resource as such to accommodate vast offshore constructions. Extensive artificial islands rising from the seabed, the stuff of pipe-dreams a few years ago, are now massive silhouettes against the seascape and the sky. One such is the island built by Nippon Kokan, one kilometre off shore, to take an entire integrated steel works. This island of Ohgishima

---

[7] The Sea Fisheries (Shellfish) Act, 1967, is the main statute. As at September 1982, there were 29 statutory orders under the 1967 Act granting several or regulated fisheries in England and Wales.

[8] The site was the riverbed of the Colne owned by Colchester Borough Council.

[9] Annotated Code of Maryland: Natural Resources Article, *Title 4, Fish and Fisheries*, 4-1114.

not only has its foundations in the seabed but is the site of a submarine tunnel joining it to the mainland.[10] The development is indicative of the extensive demands on the seabed which off-shore civil engineering will make in the future.

In Europe, activity in the Netherlands is becoming more intensive. The Dutch Delta programme is responsible for the massive off-shore construction of Europort and other projects. There have recently been serious discussions about a huge artificial island on the Dutch continental shelf to take heavy industry and relieve the mainland. A new law[11] is now ready to transfer the government of the seabed and the approach waters (1 kilometre out from the land) from the Crown Domain to local coastal authorities; in consequence, plans are being mounted for a seabed housing estate off Scheveningen. Local Acts of Parliament in Britain, such as the Brighton Marina Act of 1968 and the Zetland County Council Act of 1974, are becoming more frequent and are intended to support the development of the seabed by local authorities and private companies. Harbour and port authorities in Britain – which, as a general rule, do not own the seabed under the waters over which they have navigational jurisdiction – today encounter resistance from the Crown to requests for the acquisition of fee-simple estates in the seabed of the harbours, although in the past the attitude of the Crown had been more liberal.

We are not concerned here with the policies and politics behind these activities and legislation; we merely record them as important evidence of the growing demand for ownership of the seabed resource.

Oil and mining companies

There is no legal, practical or constitutional reason why oil and mining companies should not own absolute rights in mineral-bearing land. Landowners who were neither miners nor oil men nevertheless wanted their mineral wealth worked and won whilst retaining their land titles in perpetuity. The mining lease and oil licence were devices employed to resolve conflicts of land ownership and land use. The seabed is likely to be freer of such tensions in many respects. Given that the price was right, oil and mining companies would most

---

[10] The Japanese refer to such developments as 'the city-on-the-sea programme'. (*NKK Today*, published by Nippon Kokan, Tokyo, 1982).

[11] Municipal Division of The Waddensee, Ph. 119/1q/4, 1983; and Memo. DG BB2 /TA/Disk88.

probably find considerable advantage in owning the mineral-bearing resource. The experience of the British National Coal Board in acquiring estates in the surface land of the coal mines bears out the benefits of merging the proprietary interests. An absolute title, with the freedom of sale and alienation it confers, should be more acceptable than licences issued by an international authority to the international consortia[12] (considered below, pp. 73-74) set up by private firms and governments to mine the deep ocean bed.

Moreover, the oil companies are increasingly installing plant on the seabed in the form of more or less permanent structures. Like the civil engineering works mentioned above, these installations should be supported by appropriate interests in the seabed of long duration or in perpetuity.

Examples of such structures are the off-shore terminals to accommodate today's massive tankers, fixed production platforms, extensive underwater chambers associated with subsea systems, and the million-barrel storage tanks now in place in the North Sea, Persian Gulf and other areas.

Nevertheless, oil companies are oil companies and, as such, might be wary of property rights—whether as licensees, lessees or holders of less limited interests—which involved them in responsibilities beyond oil production. If absolute ownership or a freehold estate in the seabed resource meant additional responsibilities – activities and costs beyond oil production – the demand for such property interests could be affected. A special feature of seabed practice, however, has been the granting of licences to consortia whose members are not specialist oil companies. In the North Sea in 1979-80, for example, seaward production licences were held not only by oil companies but by banks, brewers, publishers, property companies and the chemical industry.[13] So wide a spectrum of commerce and business could find the ownership of interests in the seabed resource an attraction.

Dredging companies

Of all the operators active on the seabed at the present time, the dredging companies are the most immediately in physical contact

[12] The consortia are: Kennecott Consortium; Ocean Mining Associates; Ocean Management Incorporated; Ocean Minerals Company; Association française pour l'étude et la recherche des nodules (AFERNOD); Deep Ocean Minerals Association (DOMA).
[13] *Continental Shelf Act 1964: Report for Year 1979-80*, HC 785, HMSO, 29 October 1980.

with it over relatively extensive areas. The marine dredging industry has two distinct sides: one is contractual, the dredging of the sea bottom to obtain 'fill' for a specific purpose or to cut away banks and rock formations; the other dredges for saleable deposits of sand, gravel and rock. There are technical reasons, based on the British experience, for thinking that environmental and navigational hazards might be reduced if the practice of issuing *ad hoc* licences gave way to the acquisition of private legal estates in the seabed. Current official records of dredging facilities granted in the territorial sea and on the continental shelf of Britain to companies marketing sand and gravel aggregates suggest that that side of the industry would not be indifferent to an open market in the seabed resource.

The British Government is actively encouraging dredging. Not only do these submarine operations relieve pressure on the land; they also contribute to exports.[14] There is expansion also in other countries. The US Department of the Interior offered leases for sand and gravel dredging on the outer continental shelf for the first time in 1983. Recent surveys by the Geological Survey of Lower Saxony have revealed sand and gravel deposits in the German off-shore zone which could double national supplies. And in the coastal areas of Belgium some five sand and gravel concessions are already operating.

Other activities

To the list of those who could be making property claims on the seabed resource in the future it would be reasonable to add the engineering firms and operators who will be making available for industrial and other uses the thermal and mechanical energies of the seas. Massive structures will be required, widely varying in form and function but all demanding anchorage on the seabed or exclusive sites in the waters. Writing recently about ocean energy, Dr Walter R. Schmitt made the pertinent observation that some platforms may in time be moved into international waters for years on end.[15]

A market in the seabed resource would also have to accommodate

---

[14] In recent years, the production of sand and gravel in the UK has been over 100 million tonnes a year; 11-13 million tonnes are raised annually from the seabed and an additional 3-4 million tonnes are marine-dredged and exported. (*UK Mineral Statistics*, HMSO, 1981.)

[15] Schmitt, *op. cit.*, p. 85.

the vast, intricate weave and web of pipelines, cables and other servicing gear required to link off-shore plants to each other and to the landfalls. Demands for wayleaves, easements, and even corporate interests in the seabed for these installations must be anticipated.

On land, property companies as developers and investors supply commercial and industrial undertakings with the land and buildings they require. The services of a property market are thus made available to industry and commerce by these specialised intermediary activities. Once an open property market has been established over the seabed resource, it would be reasonable to expect property companies and developers to contribute substantially to the general demand.

(iii) *Thrust of technology*

Applied science and the creative genius of modern technology are the prime movers behind the present development of the seabed, and there is no new thrust in demand which will not be dependent upon advances in these realms of knowledge. New ideas and innovations have taken and will continue to take the lead in demands for the seabed resource. Economically, the seabed is inert without the technologist, in a way the land never was. Thus, to the question of who wants the seabed resource, an important part of the answer is: those who will encourage, finance and use the innovators and their novel ideas.

Once under the water, getting oil, gas and minerals and utilising the seabed itself as a foundation for industrial development, the aim of the technologist is to find what he calls 'enhanced recovery methods' to operate at ever-greater depths. As a consequence, the demands for use and possession of the seabed resource have continuously expanded. All evidence points to the trends of the past being but forerunners of the trends of the foreseeable future. With oil, the aim is to get into the deeper fathoms, to improve the means of bulk storage under the seas, to give more capacity and speed to shipment and off-loading, and to enlarge and make more effective on-shore and off-shore conveyance, production and refining.

The same principle holds with mining. Scientific knowledge and skills, together with the finance to promote and exploit them, can be beyond the capacity of even the largest mining corporations. Even to contemplate getting at and lifting the polymetallic nodules from the deep-ocean bed, over 5,000 metres down, has meant the pooling of resources and assets and the creation of international consortia of unprecedented size.[16] Yet such amalgamations have taken place, and the advance in the experiments and their outcome have their message for any future market in the seabed resource. On a less spectacular scale, aggregates are being dredged at depths which a few years ago were well beyond the reach of the dredging craft. Technology goes relentlessly ahead and it seems that only economic considerations will impose limits on what can be done – as happens when the marginal reward to the capital employed in providing the technology does not justify the investment. A dredger working at new operating depths can today cost £6½ million – no mean sum for an industry whose gross profit margins are very narrow.

Even in the realm of sedentary fisheries, technology is opening up the range of possibilities. The naturally-bred oyster, for example, is now being replaced by broods from hatcheries, a process which can feed the planter with a near-endless supply of stock and thus multiply the number of oyster farms.

Improvements in techniques are only one side of the technological advances to be anticipated. The new-ideas shop is also open, active and ambitious. Experiments in aquaculture and especially the near-breakthroughs in energy conversion promise an expanding demand for access rights over the seabed resource in one form or another. And, let it be remembered, we are still only in the very early days of seabed experiment and exploitation.

Transfer of technology

On a global scale, demands for access to the seabed which follow the advance of technology will be uneven and patchy. Western nations, especially the USA, have the know-how. The benefit and demand consequent upon its use are not available today to nations too poor to buy it and insufficiently trained to operate it.

Demands from the developing nations, though potentially vast, are in practice likely to be limited. Patterns in the future will be fashioned largely by the extent to which technology is transferred to them from the advanced countries. An entire part of the Law of the Sea Conven-

---

[16] Above, p. 24, note 12.

tion (Part XIV) is devoted to prescribing obligations and aims for the development and transfer of marine technology. Article 268 spells out the basic objectives as, *inter alia*:

'(a) the acquisition, evaluation and dissemination of marine technological knowledge and [to] facilitate access to such information and data;
(b) the development of appropriate marine technology;
(c) the development of the necessary technological infrastructure to facilitate the transfer of marine technology.'

More generally, the UN has for some years striven to establish an International Code of Conduct on Transfer of Technology,[17] and currently has one in draft form.[18] All such international initiatives to promote and disseminate marine technology and to strengthen the capacity of the developing countries to participate will have a decisive effect – albeit an indirect one – on the scale of demands for access to and ownership of the seabed resource in the medium and longer term. A bilateral agreement for the transfer of technology, freely entered into between a developed and a developing nation, should be distinguished from the mandatory transfer of technology which the ISA, in the exercise of its collective sovereignty, will demand as part of the price of allowing access to the resources of the deep-ocean bed.[19]

---

[17] UN Resolution 1713 (XVI) of 19 December 1961.

[18] UNCTAD, *Draft International Code of Conduct on Transfer of Technology*, TD/CODE TOT/33, 12 May 1981.

[19] Below, pp. 36–37.

IV. Who Holds It?

Zones and Jurisdictions

A market in the seabed resource, like any other market, has to be supplied. Someone, therefore, must have the right to dispose of interests in the resource by sale. This is to say, in effect, that someone must *own* the interests in the seabed resource, for the right of disposal is one of the basic constituents of ownership.[1] The power to sanction the ownership by either public bodies or private persons of interests in land lies with the state which has territorial sovereignty and jurisdiction over the resource. Out on the seabed, beyond the range of national jurisdiction and in the no-man's-land which the international lawyers call *territorium nullius*, it would be legal for anyone to sink an oil well, establish a mine site, or commit some other act of overt possession and, on the grounds of that action, claim rights of ownership in the resource.[2] But unless the state of which the operators were nationals recognised and upheld their interests, they would have considerable difficulty in even bringing their claims before an international court, let alone defending them.

In recent times, international law has changed its attitude towards the individual. In contrast to earlier days, people and private institutions are now recognised as subjects of international law, but they

'lack the procedural capacity to espouse their claims before international tribunals and such claims can be entertained only at the instance of the State of which the individual is a national . . .'.[3]

This lesson was painfully learnt in 1974 by Deep Sea Ventures Inc. Having discovered a deposit of manganese nodules 1,000 miles off

---

[1] D. R. Denman, *Place of Property*, Geographical Publications, Berkhamsted, Herts., 1978, p. 30.

[2] Such a claim would not be upheld in respect of any area of the waters of the high seas which by customary international law are *res extra commercium* (i.e., 'things that are not traded in').

[3] M. Sorensen, *Manual of Public International Law*, Macmillan, 1968, pp. 249, 265-66.

California, the company laid claim to exclusive mining rights[4] over 60,000 square kilometres of seabed and called upon the US Government to recognise and protect its interests. The US Department of State replied that it

> 'does not grant or recognise exclusive mining rights to mineral resources of the seabed beyond the limits of national jurisdiction'.

This lesson is of supreme importance for the purposes of this *Hobart Paperback*. It tells us that, before we can profitably discuss the prospects for the ownership of interests in the seabed resource and for the operation of a resource market, we must know something about the fundamentals of national sovereignty and jurisdiction over the seabed and the seas. Passing references have already been made to the division of the seas into specific and varying realms of jurisdiction. The carve-up is largely the work of conferences convened by the member states of the UN. The divisions – defined but not, in every case, agreed upon or ratified so far – are: the territorial sea and contiguous zone; the exclusive economic zone; the continental shelf; the continental margin; the Area; and exclusive fishing zones. With the exception of the Area, they are all coastal bands varying in width and measured outwards from the low-tide mark or, where circumstances require, from straight baselines drawn across bays and other indentations.[5] The critical differences are variations in jurisdiction.

Territorial sea

The notion that the sovereignty of a nation extends outwards over its territorial sea to a range of three nautical miles from the low-water mark (that is, the range of a cannon shot) has long been accepted among maritime nations. The UN Convention which formally defined the territorial sea[6] set no outward limit. UNCLOS III, however, has prescribed a maximum width of 12 nautical miles.[7] Many

---

[4] 'Deep Sea Ventures Inc. asserted the exclusive rights to develop, evaluate and mine the deposit and to recover, take, use and sell all the manganese nodules therein and the minerals and metals derived therefrom. The company did not make a specific territorial claim to the seabed.' (Opinion of the Law Offices of Northcutt Ely, *International Law Applicable to Deep Sea Mining*, submitted to Deep Sea Ventures Inc., 14 November 1974.)

[5] For the British baselines, The Territorial Waters Order in Council, 1964.

[6] Convention on the Territorial Sea and Contiguous Zone: UN. Doc. A/CONF.13/L.52, 28 April 1958.

[7] Convention on the Law of the Sea, adopted 30 April 1982; Sec. I, Article 3.

countries, claiming the consensus view of UNCLOS III as evidence of established usage, have already abandoned the three-mile limit and declared territorial seas of 12 miles. Others with less conscience, like Tanzania, have pushed their territorial sea out to 50 miles – though some Latin American states went to the extreme of 200 miles as long ago as the 1940s.[8]

The only limitation on the sovereignty and jurisdiction of a coastal state over its territorial sea and the seabed below it and the air space above it is the obligation to allow foreign ships the right of innocent passage through the waters.

Contiguous zone

The idea of a contiguous zone has been present since the Territorial Sea Convention of 1958. It is a buffer band of water, limited by UNCLOS III to 24 nautical miles from the baselines,[9] which gives a right of control to the coastal state to prevent the infringement of specified laws and to police and punish offenders.

Continental shelf

Sovereign rights,[10] albeit limited to exploring and exploiting the natural resources of the continental shelf, were recognised as being among the jurisdictions of coastal states by the Convention on the Continental Shelf of 1958.[11] The Convention defined the continental shelf as the seabed and subsoil of the submarine areas adjacent to the coast and outside the territorial sea to a depth of 200 metres or, beyond that limit, to where the depth of the superjacent waters admits of the exploitation of natural resources. This indeterminate limit has been hardened by UNCLOS III[12] to the outer edge of the continental margin or a distance of 200 nautical miles from the baselines, provided the outer edge of the continental margin is within 350 nautical miles of the baselines; if not, the outer limit is set at that distance.[13] (The UK limits are shown in Figure 1.)

---

[8] Admiralty Publications, *Annual Notice to Mariners*, No. 12, 24 July 1982, from UK Hydrographer to the Navy.

[9] *Loc. cit.*, Article 33.

[10] The formula 'sovereign rights' was used deliberately to preclude full 'sovereignty'. (See note 30 below, p. 39.)

[11] UN.Doc.A/CONF.13/L.55.

[12] *Loc. cit.*, Article 76.

[13] An alternative is 100 nautical miles from the 2,500-metre isobath, which is a line connecting points where the depth of the water measures 2,500 metres.

Continental margin

The continental margin is the incline of sediments which runs under the sea from the land face to the oceanic rock floor of the deep ocean and is divided into the shelf, the slope and the rise (Figure 2). Although the definition of the continental shelf has been tightened up, the sovereignty enjoyed by coastal states has not been altered since the 1958 Convention.

Exclusive economic zone

The sovereign rights over the continental shelf prescribed by the 1958 Convention have in practice proved too restrictive. They leave the living resources in the waters out of account, and make no provision for conservation and management or for harnessing the energies of the sea. Consequently, UNCLOS III has introduced the idea of an 'exclusive economic zone' (EEZ),[14] which will extend 200 miles outwards from the baselines. Within the EEZ, the coastal state will have sovereign rights which make good the omissions mentioned above and which also – as with the continental shelf – govern all activities involving installations and structures.

Where the continental shelf is itself contained within an EEZ, the rights over the latter will be dominant. Over the area of a continental shelf which runs beyond the outer boundary of an EEZ, sovereign rights will be normal, but operators exploiting it will be required to make payments to the ISA from their profitable operations with non-living resources.[15]

All states have the right to lay submarine cables and pipelines both on the continental shelf and within EEZs.

As with the proposed extensions of the territorial sea, certain countries have anticipated the coming into force of the Law of the Sea Convention and have unilaterally established areas which have all the characteristics of the proposed EEZs; Iceland is an example.[16] Although not a signatory to the Law of the Sea Convention, the USA has formally declared an EEZ.[17] Countries which have not yet gone to the extreme of setting up an EEZ around their coasts have moved a

---

[14] *Loc. cit.,* Part V.

[15] *Loc. cit.,* Article 82.

[16] Law No. 41 of 1 June 1979 concerning the Territorial Sea, the Economic Zone and the Continental Shelf.

[17] Proclamation of 10 March 1983 by the President of the United States.

Figure 1
CONTINENTAL SHELF UK
Designated Areas

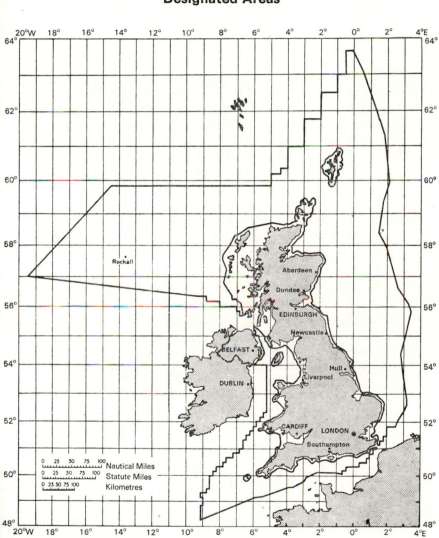

Source: Department of Energy, *Continental Shelf Act, 1964: Report for Year 1980–81,* HC466, HMSO, 1981.

quarter of the way by drawing the bounds of fishery zones. These are
areas within which fishing is exclusive to the coastal state plus any
foreign fishing boats the state may permit. Many countries had
already pushed out their fishery zones to coincide with what will
eventually be the boundaries of their EEZs.[18]

The Common Heritage of Mankind

Under international customary law, so long as no state has *bona fide*
jurisdiction over an area of the seabed (as distinct from the waters of
the high seas), any other state can harvest its resources and, in certain
circumstances, acquire an exclusive title in them together with
sovereignty over the area. The process is similar to colonisation, where
sovereignty would follow settlement. There is a logical justice in the
law as it so stands. Those who are able and willing to be pioneers and
risk-takers have first claim to the virgin lands they discover or to the
unclaimed seabed they exploit. This would still be the final word on
determining sovereignty and ownership of the seabed resource of the
deep ocean lying beyond all national jurisdictions had not the UN
solemnly declared, on 17 December 1970, that

'(a) the seabed and ocean floor, and the subsoil thereof, beyond the limits
of national jurisdiction (referred to as the Area) as well as the resources
of the Area, are the common heritage of mankind;

(b) the Area shall not be subject to appropriation by any means by States
or persons, natural or juridical, and no State shall claim or exercise
sovereignty or sovereign rights over any part thereof.'[19]

The spirit and intention of that Declaration lived on to be embodied
in the UN Charter of Economic Rights and Duties of States in 1974
and, ultimately, in the Law of the Sea Convention. The Convention[20]
acknowledges the common heritage of mankind over the resources
of the deep-ocean bed. This it terms the Area, gives it a legal status
and sets up an unprecedented, autocratic International Seabed Authority, implicitly invested with sovereignty and absolute jurisdiction, to
rule over it, in the name of all mankind. The Convention has been

[18] Examples of legislation are the US Fishery Conservation and Management Act, 1976,
and the UK Fishery Limits Act, 1976.
[19] *Declaration of Principles Governing the Seabed and the Ocean Floor and the Subsoil thereof
beyond the limits of National Jurisdiction*: A/RES/2749 (XXV), 17 December 1970.
[20] Part XI.

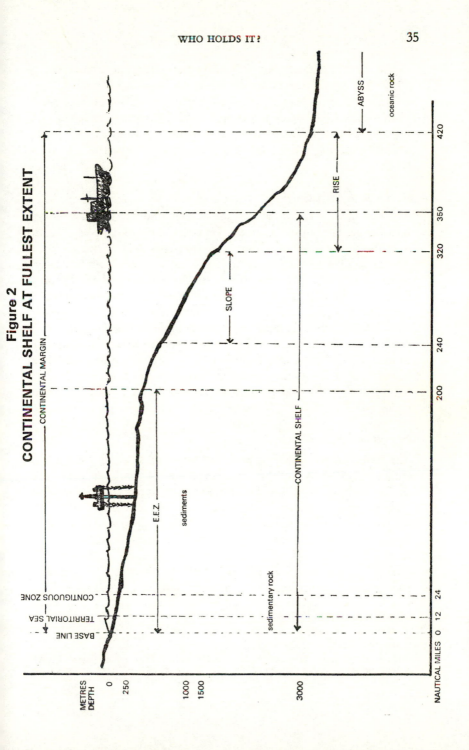

Figure 2

CONTINENTAL SHELF AT FULLEST EXTENT

signed by 125 nations, but only three had ratified it by the end of
1983 – Fiji, Mexico and Jamaica.

Thus, though conceived, the new 'giant' has still to be brought to
birth. International opinion is deeply divided for and against a healthy
delivery. Numerically, however, support for it is sufficiently weighty
to justify making a more detailed examination of the ISA and all its
works.

Tenure to be challenged

The notion of a common heritage of mankind fits happily enough
into the social philosopher's tool kit as a theory of property. It also
strengthens the case of those who advocate a New International
Economic Order, and it is perhaps not incongruous with the Outer
Space Treaty[21] and the Agreement on the Moon,[22] where it found
early expression, or as a criterion justifying the *terra communis* status of
Antarctica[23] – as a territory only for international scientific research
and discovery. But there are rational grounds for challenging it as a
workable mode of tenure. The attempt to give expression to it appears
to lead the UN itself into commerce in a way its Charter can never
have intended. We shall consider the implications of this later (pp. 56-
59), after first examining in detail how the ISA is to be run and
equipped.

International monopoly

The International Seabed Authority[24] will consist of all states which
are parties to the Law of the Sea Convention and will operate through
an Assembly of its members. The power of effective policy-making
will rest with a Council of 36 nations whose constitution, however,
is not destined to represent adequately those countries which will be
required to contribute the larger share of the finances and skill to the
work of the ISA and which will probably be most affected by the
decisions of the Council. The ISA will have supreme monopolistic
powers (the biggest monopoly on earth) over the licensing and dis-

---

[21] Outer Space Treaty, 1967, Article 2.

[22] Agreement Governing the Activities of States on the Moon, 1979, Article 11.

[23] Antarctica Treaty, 1961, Article IV-2.

[24] The brief description of the organisation and functions of the ISA given here is taken
from the provisions of Part XI, Articles 133-191, of the Convention on the Law of
the Sea open for signature in Jamaica from December 1982.

position of resources[25] in the Area – that is, over something like 60 per cent of the area of the globe. Not only is the ISA to be the paramount administrative power in the deep oceans, it is also required to set up its own operating corporation, called the Enterprise. The only activities which will be permitted in the Area will be carried out either by the Enterprise or by states, private persons and companies working in association with the ISA through 'plans of work' in the form of contracts approved by the Council.

Who shall prospect, explore and exploit the Area will be for the ISA to decide. Even prospectors, doing no more than scanning the scene, will have to operate under the eye of the Authority which will verify whether they are complying with the provisions of the Convention. While the Enterprise will be free to operate anywhere in the Area, all other operators – those who, at the outset, will inevitably be the financiers of the ISA and the processors of know-how, training facilities and capital – will be barred from 'reserved areas'. Moreover, the ISA will have the authority to

'take measures necessary to promote the growth, efficiency and stability of markets for those commodities produced from the minerals derived from the Area, at prices remunerative to producers and fair to consumers'.[26]

To this end it will enter into commodity agreements, work to a ceiling for nickel production (and probably ceilings for other minerals), and trim its policies for authorising production to its global commitments.

Each application for approval will have to be made for a site which can be divided into two of equal commercial value. One of the two, at the discretion of the ISA, will be reserved for the Enterprise. Having in this way 'found' the Enterprise a site, the operator, if he is to be approved by the ISA, must further contract to make available to the Enterprise or to a developing country, or group of countries, on fair and reasonable terms and conditions, 'the technology which he uses in carrying out activities in the Area'.

The state or private concern which submits to these demands will have to bear additional heavy financial burdens in favour of the ISA. In brief, these will be: an initial fee of US $500,000; an annual fee of

---

[25] Resources are defined in this context as 'all solid, liquid or gaseous mineral resources *in situ* in the Area at or beneath the seabed, including polymetallic nodules'.

[26] UNCLOS III, Part XI, Article 151 (1a).

US $1 million; and a high production charge which could eventually
amount to 12 per cent of the market value of the processed metals or,
alternatively, a smaller charge of 4 per cent plus a share of the net
proceeds of the operator's enterprise, which could rise at the margin
to 70 per cent.[27]

A contradiction

The irony of this centralised and collectivist world scheme, with its
built-in controls and discrimination in favour of the Enterprise and
certain countries which are to be given privileged access to 'reserve'
sites, is inescapable. For the whole apparatus is purported to be created
and motivated for the benefit of all mankind, as the proud patron of
a 'common heritage' which is nowhere defined and lies beyond the
wit of practical men to understand. The Convention as it now stands,[28]
signed by 125 nations, is patently not the unanimous voice of mankind
as a whole. Yet its Article 137 provides that 'all rights in the resources
of the Area are vested in mankind as a whole, on whose behalf
the Authority shall act'. Mankind 'as a whole' must surely include
the peoples of those countries which have been unwilling to sign the
Convention. Thus we are faced with the contradiction of one part of
mankind claiming title in common with the rest of mankind to property
which the latter disowns. Mankind as a whole has given no power of
attorney to the parties to the Law of the Sea Convention. How could
it do so? Mankind as a whole has no voice, no unitary consciousness
and no international personality.

Ownership and Property Rights

At this stage we should remind ourselves of our objective. We are
looking for signs of an actual or potential market in the seabed resource.
We want to know, therefore, who holds property rights in the seabed
because only proprietors can supply the market.

'So with the seas, as with the land'

International treaties on the seabed, and the divisions and boundary
disputes to which they give rise, are debated among states. Claims

---

[27] A penetrating critique of the status, power and functions of the ISA appears in the 'Statement made on 23 June 1982 before the Foreign Affairs Committee of the House of
Representatives by Northcutt Ely of Law Offices of Northcutt Ely, Washington DC'.
[28] Autumn 1983.

and allocations are justified by reference to sovereign rights or, simply, jurisdiction. Property rights and ownership *per se* are not at issue among states. They are nevertheless there, insistent and importunate, in the background, ultimately dependent upon the sovereignties and jurisdictions. In earlier days, a prince or head of state would exercise sovereignty over the land and water of his realm so as to vest property rights and ownership in himself and his subjects. Ownership, as the jurists maintained, lay in *dominium*, subsumed under sovereignty (*imperium*). In England, the courts had for centuries debated how far the king's sovereignty stretched over the seas.[29] Some jurists contended that the royal writ and realm stopped at the low-water mark. Others, with whom today's verdict seems to agree, argued for nothing less than the width of the territorial sea and saw in the king's sovereignty the source of both jurisdiction and ownership. As the lord of the Great Waste, the sea, the sovereign inherited both the waters and their land (seabed). There was no division between them: *tam aquae quam soli*.

'So with the seas, as with the land' was well enough said in the days when no-one thought of the seabed as a realm of riches in its own right. Modern thinking and laws, however, have divided not only seas from seas but also the waters from the seabed. Basic to the Law of the Sea Convention is the principle that sovereign rights over the natural resources of the seabed of the continental shelf must not be exercised so as to infringe the freedom of the high seas.[30] The same principle will apply to the wider sovereign rights in the EEZs and even in the deep oceans.

The practical question arises, therefore, whether these sovereign rights, as distinct from full sovereignty (*imperium*), are sufficient to sanction property rights (*dominium*). Different countries use different phrases to denote the command their respective governments exercise over the natural resources of the continental shelf. Belgium and the Netherlands refer to 'sovereign rights', the UK and Norway to 'rights' and 'the right'; Denmark's law states that the natural resources

---

[29] Geoffrey Marston, *The Marginal Seabed: United Kingdom Legal Practice*, Clarendon Press, Oxford, 1981.

[30] The term 'sovereign rights' was used in the earlier conventions to limit the exercise of national sovereignty to the seabed and to exclude sovereignty in the superjacent waters. (M. S. McDougal and W. T. Burke, *The Public Order of the Oceans*, Yale University Press, 1962, pp. 694-703.)

'belong to the Danish state';[31] and France imposes '*un régime juridique unique*' over the continental shelf.[32] In no instance is the right or power of property conferred, vested, or even mentioned. However, Norway's Royal Decree of 8 December 1972, on the exploration for and exploitation of petrol in the seabed of the continental shelf carries an indirect reference. The Decree applies to the internal waters, territorial seas and continental shelf but not to areas 'subject to private property rights'.[33] This exclusion of private property from the run of the Decree stems from the national customary law which recognises private property in the seabed out from the low-water mark to a depth of two metres – the height of a man standing. The British Offshore Petroleum Development (Scotland) Act of 1975[34] indirectly mentions 'private rights in the sea or seabed', but not specifically private property.

In the USA, the subsoil and seabed of the outer continental shelf 'appertain' to the United States.[35] Case law in that country, however, is more definite in its views. There are four leading cases: *USA v. California*, 1947; *USA v. Louisiana*, 1950; *USA v. Texas*, 1950; *USA v. Maine et al.*, 1975. All were brought by the Federal Government against States which claimed jurisdiction and ownership of the seabed in the marginal sea and continental shelf. Texas and Louisiana in particular claimed *dominium* and *imperium*. It was alleged in the Texas case that the USA was

> 'the owner in fee simple of, or possessed of paramount rights in, and full dominium and power over, the lands, minerals and other things underlying the Gulf of Mexico, lying seaward of the ordinary low-water mark on the coast of Texas and outside of the inland waters, extending seaward to the outer edge of the continental shelf . . .'[36]

Competence to create property

The best we can do is to conclude from the evidence of accepted – albeit very recent – practice and usage that 'sovereign rights' over a

---

[31] Law texts cited and translated in Appendix IV to *The North Sea Challenge and Opportunity*, Europa Publications, London, 1975.

[32] Art. ler., Titre Premier, Loi No. 68-1181 of 30 December 1968.

[33] Chapter 1, Section 1.

[34] Section 5(3).

[35] Outer Continental Shelf Lands Act, 1953, Section 2(a).

[36] 94.L.ed. 1222, October Term, 1949.

continental shelf, within the meaning of the UN Continental Shelf Convention of 1958, bestow on the states empowered to exercise them competence to create derivative property rights (leases) and quasi-property rights (licences) out of them for the benefit of both public and private holders. This use of the power of sovereign rights has a most important and immediate significance for a resource market. We may infer from it that the state has a kind of *dominium* or property right – an ownership in the seabed from which valid lesser rights are derived and can be alienated. Who can say whether that *dominium* itself can or cannot be granted to another in exchange for a price or *bona fide* consideration?

When, earlier in this *Hobart Paperback*, the functions of a land market were described (pp. 5-7), it was pointed out that, in one way or another, the market deals in rights rather than in land, the natural *solum* itself. It follows, therefore, that the creation of derivative rights in the seabed from the superior title (*dominium*) of the state is an act supplying a property market in the seabed resource, however restricted and dominated by the state monopoly that market may be. And any evidence that the absolute title of the Crown or state in the seabed resource of territorial waters has itself been granted or conveyed to other owners suggests even more strongly that there is an effective supply of private property, however tiny. In the light of these general observations, it is possible to detect from particular examples clear signs of an incipient resource market, albeit a much restricted one.

Forms of ownership

Forms of resource ownership can be broadly classified as communal or individual, and absolute or derivative.[37] There is already evidence of all these classes in the proprietary pattern of the seabed resource. In many countries, each citizen has a right, in common with his neighbour, to fish the territorial waters – a right which finds a counterpart in the inter-commoning[38] of states and their nationals on the high seas. Common rights in a limited resource, freely enjoyed by an unlimited number of commoners, lead sooner or later to an ever-dwindling marginal return to capital and other inputs employed in

---

[37] D. R. Denman, *op. cit.*, pp. 101-120.

[38] The term 'inter-commoning' refers to the exercise of rights by commoners where two or more adjacent commons abut or overlap each other.

their use, and eventually to the exhaustion of the common resource. For this reason, the principle of an exclusive right is introduced on economic grounds. The establishment of exclusive fishery zones in coastal waters is an example, as also is the granting of exclusive individual rights in severalty over the seabed for shellfish culture under the British Sea Fisheries (Shellfish) Act of 1967. This policy, though ordained by Parliament and conducted under statute in Britain, is hampered because the recipients of the grant have to obtain the agreement of the owner of the seabed to the establishment of the several fisheries – and this usually means getting the agreement of the Crown Estate Commissioners. An exclusive right is of the utmost importance to the development of a resource market. There can be no market in something which is free for all. Once exclusively possessed, however, that something becomes scarce and scarcity generates value. In the market, value determines price – a process that we shall be examining later (p. 49).

Monopoly derived from an absolute property right vested in the state or Crown over the seabed resource of territorial waters is commonplace among nations. It is, however, by no means always entire and unbreached. The presence of private property in the Norwegian coastal waters, for example, has already been noted. And Britain provides some colourful examples. There, the Crown's title to the foreshore and the seabed of internal and territorial waters runs back over the centuries, parallel with the course of the common law. But, all round the coast, instances occur of private and local government ownership breaking into the Crown title. Many go back to ancient grants – as with the title to parts of the seabed now vesting in the Seasalter Shellfish Co. Ltd. in Whitstable, the 15th-century Royal Charter which vested the seabed of the Medway in the burgesses of Rochester, and the extensive grants by Henry IV of the Lordship of Man to John de Stanley in 1405. There are also titles won from the Crown by prescriptive claims based on long usage. In other instances, the Royal title was never acknowledged. The breach is spectacular here and there, notably in the case of Bembridge Harbour in the Isle of Wight.[39] Now in the hands of a private company, ownership of the seabed and its minerals stretches out beyond the harbour. The sheer force of demand generated by industrial and commercial development, and more particularly by the building of great harbours and

---

[39] Below, pp. 54-55.

seaworks, has induced the Crown, with the sanction of Parliament, to convey title in the seabed to harbour boards and port authorities.[40]

The most prolific source of property rights in the seabed of territorial waters and the continental shelf under the high seas has been the granting of derivative interests, carved out of the superior title of the state or Crown and varying in type. These derivatives tend to fall into two classes – leases and licences. Under the land law of England and its American parallel, a lease has a property status similar to real property; a leasehold interest can be owned and held as a chattel-real.[41] A licence is more personal, like a servitude. For practical purposes, however, a licence has all the characteristics of a lease. In Britain leases are granted in the seabed of the territorial sea, but nothing grander than a licence is granted in the continental shelf. In America, oil production leases are granted irrespective of the divisions between outer and inner continental shelves and territorial waters. They are the stock form of private property and are more readily available than are the licences in Britain and other countries.

Wherever they are granted, these derivative forms of property in the seabed resource exist in supine dependence upon the state monopolistic reversioner. Because the reversioner is the state, the grantees have little, if any, bargaining power. Those who want leases and licences have to negotiate terms knowing that there are no alternative grantors to turn to. The state monopolist can adopt a take-it-or-leave-it attitude; and selection is wholly at his discretion. In Britain and most other countries except America, the relevant department of state has handed out licences to successful candidates selected arbitrarily at its discretion. In America, the practice is to 'auction' the seabed lease through a tender scheme which accepts the highest bid. Five-year exploration leases are followed by production leases, although the lessee of the former can be outbid in the market when competing for a production lease. Production leases are indeterminate, running for as long as the lessee thinks it profitable to operate the leased property. In current practice in seabed development, these leases are the nearest thing to private ownership of the seabed resource in perpetuity.

All leases, unlike licences, convey ownership of what the land law calls 'limited interests'. An interest is limited because its time-span

---

[40] Cf. above, pp. 22-23.
[41] Cheshire, *op. cit.*, p. 38.

is fixed in some way. Usually, a lease runs for a fixed term of years, though some run on from year to year until terminated by one or other party. Ownership of an 'estate' or 'interest of unlimited duration' is the nearest thing under English law to absolute ownership of the land. It follows that a lease, such as the American production lease which is open-ended and continues at the discretion of the lessee, comes very near in character to a perpetual estate. Normally, the longer the duration of a lease, the higher its price (premium or bonus) in the property market. This is reflected in the American practice of limiting the maximum size of the leased area to 5,760 acres so as to keep the price of the leased tract within the bidding range of a wide market.[42] The American way has an important message for us. It conforms the closest to an open market in the seabed resource and will engage our attention again in the next section when we examine the case for or against the continuation of state monopolies over the seabed.

---

[42] US Outer Continental Shelf Lands Act, 1953, Section 8, b (1).

V. Who Should Hold It?

Mine and Yours – to Enclose

Years ago, Marshall saw capital invested to 'improve' land as being embodied in it and yielding *quasi-rent*, along with the rent of the land itself.[1] While the land market disregards these distinctions, it nonetheless buys up (capitalises) and trades in the right to receive rental income from land, whether in a state of nature or improved. Other things equal, and given a constant rate of yield, the higher the rental income (whether enjoyed as either actual income or an equivalent money flow or in some other form of satisfaction[2]), the larger the capital value of the land will be. And, by economic standards, the higher the open-market value of the land, the more efficient its use is likely to be.

The analogy between the land and the seabed resource which we drew at the beginning of this *Hobart Paperback* holds true for the above analysis. The analogy is apparent today, however, only because of the demand for the seabed resource. Land would yield no rent but for its scarcity. If land were a 'free good', capital and labour would work their respective wills on it, to earn interest and wages, as they do with abundant air.[3] Like free air, the seabed was there for the taking. There was no scarcity, and hence no rent.[4] All that has now changed. Claimants, hitherto unknown, are apprehending the seabed resource, apportioning it, fencing it in with boundaries of 'mine and yours', giving it an exclusiveness and, in consequence, a rent-yielding capacity. When President Truman in 1945 and all the parties to the UNLOS conferences who followed him drew national boundaries round continental shelves and economic zones and so carved up the

---

[1] Marshall, *op. cit.*, p. 349.

[2] The rental equivalent, for example, of *'personal value in current use'*. (Barry Bracewell-Milnes, *Land and Heritage: The Public Interest in Personal Ownership*, Hobart Paper 93, IEA, 1982, p. 81.)

[3] In high-density urban development, air rights generate 'rent' as the air space above buildings acquires a scarcity.

[4] This was true even though boundaries had been set to territorial waters.

45

high seas, they set the scene for a rent-yielding seabed resource. That was no bad thing. It put exclusiveness in operation, demonstrated the fact of scarcity and therefore rent, and gave the seabed value.

Boundaries do not in themselves create scarcity. Scarcity is a function of demand interacting with supply. Boundaries protect the scarce resource, making it exclusive to he who owns the resource within them. The fence enables the owner to claim payment (rent) from those who would otherwise have tried to help themselves. In other words, the land, the seabed or any other resource can yield rent only to he who exercises property rights over it. If the seabed resource is to be used and developed efficiently, it must be subject to forms of exclusive ownership. The corollary of this precondition is that we must know what form of ownership or of property right is the most efficient for the distribution and use of the seabed resource. The word 'efficient' is used here in a special sense to mean the form of ownership which will make possible the highest true rent[5] from the resource, and hence the highest value. It is acknowledged that there are other criteria for judging the use of a resource.

Mine and Yours – to Choose

The form of tenure which will satisfy the test of efficiency is one which gives the owner the highest degree of flexibility over the resource. An owner has this flexibility when he can adjust the size, shape and location of a seabed site so as to provide just what is required to accommodate the structures, plant and other items of fixed capital which he puts on the site; and, in addition, can trim the duration of the term of ownership so as to make it coincide with the profitable life of his development enterprise. An example from current policies is the production lease granted by the US Department of the Interior which runs for as long as the lessee thinks it prudent to invest and operate capital. Where the resource and the capital to develop it are in the same ownership, the degree of flexibility is likely to be highest.[6] In the normal course of events, however, so perfect a complementarity[7]

---

[5] A resource whose supply was wholly in the hands of a monopoly could be made available to tenants in consideration of the payment of 'rent' which would be true rent *plus* a proportion of the income generated by capital and labour and properly belonging to those factors.

[6] Denman, *op. cit.*, p. 31.

[7] For an examination of the complementarity of land and capital, D. R. Denman and S. Prodano, *Land Use: An Introduction to Proprietary Land Use Analysis*, George Allen and Unwin, London, 1972.

is unlikely to be accidental. It can be brought about by adjustment in one of three ways:

(i) The owner of the capital and of the resource holds too much of the latter relative to the former and disposes of the surplus to leave a residue in more or less perfect complementarity with the capital.

(ii) The owner of an estate in the resource has neither the intent nor the capital to develop it, and either disposes of the resource to developers in lots designed to suit their respective capital investments or creates derivative interests to the same end and retains a reversion in the whole resource.

(iii) The owner of the capital holds none or an insufficient amount of the resource and, to make up the short-fall, acquires an interest or a further interest in it, which could be either absolute or derivative.

In these three different ways, the resource is being either supplied or demanded to meet the needs of development and operating capital. In short, a market is in operation. The freer the market, the wider the choice; and the wider the choice, the more the customers (the owners of the development capital) are likely to be satisfied with the goods and the price. To meet these criteria, the seabed resource should be available to anyone who wished to acquire an interest in it free of restrictions on its use and development and of prohibitions against its disposal – conditions which can be perfectly met only by a tenure policy permitting unrestrained, freely-alienable private property.

Until a seabed resource market in private property was well established, purchases of estates in the seabed to be held simply for the satisfaction of ownership or general investment would probably be infrequent – although they are not unknown even at the present time.[8] Current indications suggest that, in the early stages of a full-blooded resource market, purchasers would be single-purposed, buying for oil extraction, fish farming, energy conversion, or some other specific activity. Such purchasers would demand more choice than those buying the seabed resource for speculative investment or some other general purpose.

---

[8] An example is the acquisition of the river bed of the Colne already noted (above, p. 22).

In order to function efficiently, a market in the seabed resource tuned to the requirements of its customers in these early days of experiment, innovation and uncertainty would have to be flexible, allowing the purchasers – the developers – a wide-ranging choice of lots, plots and sites. At the same time, it would be expected to offer titles to the seabed commensurate in duration at least with the life of the fixed capital equipment required for development.

Market choice – an example

Let us consider, by way of example, the present uncertainty about what constitutes an efficient deep-sea mining site.[9] The Law of the Sea Convention, with its ISA, would require a mining company to identify the area it wanted for a mine site and to offer a parallel proven site to the Enterprise. The operators would thus be forced to make assumptions about uncertainties in order to get authority to test those assumptions. In a free resource market they would be able to acquire interests in the seabed resource as intelligence about the site matured, and to dispose of surplus resource areas.[10] The acquisition of an absolute title to a seabed resource area might not be sought if the purchaser merely wanted to mine polymetallic nodules, dredge for aggregates, drill for oil or follow some other single purpose.

A free property market, functioning properly, should be able to offer exclusive and limited property rights adaptable in duration and suited to the exploration, testing and extraction processes for the exploitation of the specific resource elements. With the terms and conditions negotiated and agreed in the open market, and thereby acceptable to the operator, there would be no trace of coercion, unwarranted control or monopoly, even though it meant an inferior interest was held under a superior one. The grant of the limited interest would be but another service of the open market responding to customers' freedom of choice, and seeing to it that the maximum marginal returns to the seabed resource and to the capital employed to develop it were gained.

---

[9] *Manganese Nodules: Dimensions and Perspectives*, UNOETO publication, 1979, pp. 83-112.

[10] A recent attempt to 'open' the market in the seabed resource of the US outer continental shelf allows operators holding exploration licences to prospect over a billion acres, whereas the range was previously much narrower. (Department of the Interior, *Fact Sheet*, 2 September 1982.)

Mine and Yours – to Exchange

An open market in the seabed resource would be a safeguard against an unacceptable monopoly and an encouragement to the small investor. In addition, its transactions would mean continued change in the pattern of ownership as buyers sought sites which would best suit their capital investments. However competitive buyers may be, their bids are muffled if a monopoly controls the market and the holders of private interests are prohibited from marketing them freely. Competitive buying calls for its counterpart – competitive selling. This fundamental reciprocity is essential if monopolies are to be broken and true market prices are to rule over exchange.

Admittedly, an open market in the seabed resource could lead the larger oil companies to dominate the market and make the going difficult for the smaller operators. At the same time, however, such a market would benefit the small company by permitting it to sell the rights of successful exploration ventures to the larger companies – in a way it is barred from doing in many countries, including Britain, under the present state monopolies. The protean technology of seabed exploitation is constantly challenging the *status quo* of resource-capital ratios. A site suited to today's plant will be inadequate or too large tomorrow. Constant adjustment, of sites and their ownership, is therefore essential if investment is to continue to be efficient. Such reform, if not enforced by state intervention, must rely upon the disposal and acquisition facilities of the open market.

Yes and No to the Seabed Monopolies

It is the verdict of natural justice and of economic analysis that risk and enterprise should reap their just rewards. The pioneering oil companies which explored the seabed of the North Sea and other unknown submarine expanses in the 1960s were private operators putting men, money and the products of their engineering skills and inventive genius at risk. Simple justice would suggest that the property in the mineral-bearing seabed resources which they discovered and developed should belong to them. Admittedly, the companies were not 'international persons' as recognised by international customary law; they would therefore require their just claims to be formally recognised by a nation state. What actually happened did not follow these simple principles but was, nevertheless, of critical importance in shaping the ownership pattern of the seabed.

In neither Britain nor other similar countries – not even in America – was anything akin to absolute ownership or property rights in perpetuity vested in the deserving pioneers. At best, in American waters, they were granted leases. In Britain and most other places, a mere licence endorsed their right to explore and subsequently sanctioned production. The result, as we have seen, was to leave the superior right vested in the state governments. In this manner, the absolute monopolies over the seabed resource of the continental shelf were set up; and a similar fate awaits the seabed of the coming EEZs under the provisions of the Law of the Sea Convention.

The limited interests granted by these monopolies have, in theory, the advantage of providing security insofar as the state as their originator honours its covenants and protects the derivative titles. Thus part of what are called transaction costs is met by the state reversioner on behalf of the operators. Logically, there is no reason why similar protection should not be afforded to purchasers of freeholds or similar proprietorships from the state. So much for theory. In practice, the picture is not so simple – at any rate, not in Britain. The Crown estate and sovereignty are so extensive that present administrative arrangements are inadequate for providing the detailed attention to local matters which good estate management requires. Consequently, licensees and tenants – notably the harbour authorities – have to pay rent to the Crown and, in addition, keep a watchful eye on the Crown's interests. The lack of local management also results in the neglect of the Crown's resources and in undetected encroachments on the Crown's seabed. Many of the defects in the present system could be prevented if the harbour authorities, both public and private, were the full owners of the seabed.

There is no known evidence of any government seriously contemplating the recognition of private, supreme titles to the ownership of the seabed of a continental shelf or of an EEZ – although, as noted above (p. 40), the maritime laws and decrees of Norway recognise a general right to private property. The monopolies over the seabed of the continental shelf have come into being as if by default of rational challenge. With territorial seas of long tradition, the case was different; state or Crown monopoly – broken here and there around the coasts of Britain by private titles and the claims of boroughs and local authorities – was a logical consequence of the extension of territorial sovereignty over the near seas, with little or no economic significance.

Justifiable retention

The retention of these extensive monopolies over the seabed of the territorial waters and of the continental shelf may be justifiable on political or constitutional grounds – or, in Britain's case, on grounds of tradition and even sentiment. But their economic justification is weak. Government officials in the USA, noting that the US share of worldwide offshore production of oil and gas shrank from 21·7 per cent in 1970 to 7·6 per cent in 1980, have candidly admitted that the curtailment was due to the misguided use of the Federal Government's monopolistic proprietorship over the seabed resource of the continental shelf.[11]

A parallel can be drawn between the exploration and exploitation of the seabed and the opening-up of the frontiers of newly-discovered territory. Under Jefferson's renowned Land Ordinance of 1785 and similar legislation, the Federal Government of America held title to the Public Lands in the expansionist days in order to ensure that they were eventually conveyed fairly to private hands. If something on these lines were the objective of the seabed monopolies, all would be well and good; we could accept them whilst they discharged the task of allocation.

Wasting capital

The case for the state monopolies over the seabed faces various indictments. Fundamentally, the monopolies prevent the emergence of hidden forces ready and willing to demonstrate the dynamics of a latent market in the seabed resource. No-one can either condemn or commend the idea of a property market in the seabed resource on the basis of empirical evidence because the way to practical demonstration is blocked.

No less seriously, the state monopolies can interfere and have interfered in seabed transactions so as adversely to affect the resource-capital ratios. Let us take as an example the granting of production licences in the continental shelf. Except where leases are 'auctioned' on American lines, the state acts arbitrarily both to select those to whom it will offer rights in the seabed and to decide the terms of the grants. In Britain and elsewhere, the relevant government department

---

[11] Department of the Interior, Minerals Management Service, *Fact Sheet*, 2 September 1982.

prepares a chart showing the seabed and the seas arbitrarily chopped up into 'blocks'.[12] The oil industry and other interests are invited to apply for production licences to operate within specific blocks. The Minister in charge selects the successful applicants at his discretion.[13] Wherever the blocks are and whatever the differentials in production costs, the licences are issued for standard fees and royalty percentages. Thus the opportunity for realising the true 'rent' yielded by the oil licence is lost. Differences in unit production costs resulting from differences in sites would give one site an advantage over another – an advantage which, in an open market for leases and licences, would be reflected in the market values of the interests sold (that is, in the premiums or 'bonuses' paid for the licences and leases).

Under the Regulations[14] drawn up by the state monopoly in Britain, these differences in sites are crudely recognised by a require-ment that the operator with a well-vantaged site must devise a 'works programme' committing him to a heavier schedule of well-sinking and other capital works than that required of licensees with poorer sites. The operator is thereby forced to undertake more capital invest-ment than he might otherwise have contemplated. The extra wells may be dry and the capital in them lost.

In an open market, the operator would have bought the lease or absolute ownership in the resource for a price which capitalised its true rent in relation to the market rents and values of other interests. The purchaser would have been free to sink whatever wells pleased him in his own block. Admittedly, he would have paid a market price for the interest in the resource, a figure which might or might not have equalled or exceeded the costs of the dry wells in the 'works programme' demanded by the state monopoly. Whatever the price, however, it would have been a market quotation; and, once bought, the interest could have been re-sold in the market and the capital invested in it regained. No such reimbursement is available to the operator with the dry wells in his 'works programme'.

---

[12] *Continental Shelf Act, 1964, Report for 1980–81*, and Reference Map, HMSO, 1981.

[13] The most recent round of allocations of licences in the North Sea (the Eighth) departs in a very modest way from arbitrary practice by offering (out of a total of 184) 15 blocks in the mature oil province of the central North Sea on a tender basis – thereby subjecting the establishment of supply prices more closely to market demand. (*London Gazette*, 24 September 1982.)

[14] *The Petroleum (Production) Regulations 1982*, No. 1,000, 20 July 1982, Sch. 5, Clauses 13, 14.

Losing rent

In the early days, the British system of arbitrary selection and standard fees meant that the state lost the true rent of the seabed. It was given away.[15] Later, in order to make good the loss, three-tier taxes were levied in addition to the standard royalties. The tax revenue so raised has largely been rent in disguise. Furthermore, it has adversely affected the current cash flow of the oil producers.[16] Had the government offered absolute title or long leases in the seabed resource on the open market, the oil companies would have had to pay much more initially for their interests, but the consideration would have been a once-and-for-all cash payment. The government would have had no justification for imposing heavy and unforeseeable recurrent taxes to claw back the rent. The rent would have been capitalised in the resource price and the operators would have been able to avoid the cash-flow problems which now confront them. In a recent attempt to induce investment in new and smaller oilfields in the North Sea, the Conservative Government has exempted production licensees from making royalty payments. This puts the oil companies even more immediately at the mercy of the fiscal authorities.[17]

In 1979, the US Department of Energy sounded out the opinion of oil companies on the merits of what it called a 'net profit share system' for the acquisition of production leases in the outer continental shelf. The preponderance of industrial opinion was against profit-sharing. Preference was clearly expressed for the system of an initial cash bonus and fixed royalty which had prevailed from the beginning. The verdict substantiated the view that the oil industry would rather incur capital payments for resource interests than face recurrent outlays of rent, taxes and profit levies.[18] In Norway, licences are granted for standard fees, graduated royalties and negotiated work programmes, but the government has also reserved to itself a bargaining counter which allows for a degree of competition among applicants. Statoil, the Norwegian state oil company, takes a minimum of 51 per cent in the

[15] Peter Lilley, *North Sea Giveaway*, Bow Publications, London, January 1980; and K. W. Dam, *Oil Resources: Who Gets What How?*, University of Chicago Press, Chicago, 1976.

[16] UK Offshore Operators Association Ltd., Press Release, 27 April 1982.

[17] The Petroleum Royalties (Relief) Act, 1983.

[18] US Department of the Interior, *Compilation of Regulations Related to Mineral Resource Activities on the Outer Continental Shelf*, Vol. I of II, January 1981, pp. 1-77.

equity of private oil companies, on their being granted production licences.[19] Companies are encouraged to offer Statoil a higher share than the obligatory minimum. Differences in the proportions offered reflect a company's view of the levels of development costs between production sites. The marginal benefit of a low-cost site over a high-cost one is the capital value of the rent of the former and is an indication to the company of the proportion and value of the assets of the company which can be offered as extra shares to Statoil, so as to secure the production licence.

Development inertia

There is reason to suppose that a near-absolute and traditional state (Crown) monopoly as exists in Britain over the seabed resource of the territorial waters can lead to development inertia. The authorities tend to wait for others to make requests for concessions on the seabed. The projects are then considered and, because of the novelty of the seabed operations and the backward-looking habit of the authorities, decisions may be inhibitory. Since there are very few competitors – in the form of other owners of the seabed resource – to challenge the authorities, stagnation can result.

An example is the manner in which the authorities have recently tried to ascertain the market rental value of oyster beds leased for the new practice of oyster cultivation.[20] Tenants were required to take short tenancies on concessionary rentals and to render full details of costs and gross takings. This, apparently, was the only way the Crown could ascertain the full market rent. The tenants, however, needed to invest in fixed equipment in order to realise the true commercial potential of the oyster enterprises. Yet such investment was out of the question so long as short-term tenancies only were being offered. This impasse and restriction on development arose from the inevitable lack of evidence of true market rents which, in turn, was due to the Crown monopoly standing in the way of an open market in the seabed resource.

Very occasionally, the monopoly is challenged in a minor but effective enough way to indicate what could happen if it were removed. The story of Bembridge Harbour in the Isle of Wight is illustrative.

---

[19] Norwegian Royal Decree, 8 December 1972, Chapter 3, Section 31.
[20] Above, pp. 20-22.

The seabed of the tidal harbour and its immediate approaches on the seaward side were owned by British Rail until 1968 when ownership was transferred to the Bembridge Harbour Improvement Company, a private company. In the 15 years of private ownership, imaginative and practical management has raised revenues more than forty-fold.

Monopoly charges

Monopolistic rigidities appear in many other guises. Where an operator has to acquire a pipeline wayleave or wants a seabed site for something more substantial (e.g. a tanker terminal), he is confronted by monopoly power imposing monopoly prices. Many are the occasions when the commercial operations of the dredging industry have suffered from state monopoly over the seabed resource. Normal practice requires dredging companies engaged in the improvement of harbours or navigation approaches to find their own fill of sand, gravel and stone. In the UK, valuable contracts have been lost because the contractor had only one supplier – the Crown monopoly – to go to. An open market would have offered alternatives. If one owner of the seabed resource had been unwilling to meet the price and other conditions for a deal, other owners would have been available. In the USA until recently, dredging of this kind was wholly or mainly in the hands of the Federal military, the Corps of Engineers. The unsatisfactory consequences of two state monopolies, the army operators and the owners of the seabed, led to a nationwide investigation[21] into the functioning of the dredging market.

In Britain, Parliament has shown a commendable awareness of the effect of the Crown monopoly. In empowering the Crown Estate Commissioners in 1961 to administer the Crown estate, it specifically required them to exclude from their asking prices 'any element of monopoly value attributable to the extent of the Crown's ownership . . .'.[22] In the case of the seabed, however, where the Crown monopoly is nearly supreme and the market unique (that is, prices are in no way comparable with a true land market), who can say what open-market prices would be? Attempts are made to value particular seabed interests of the Crown but, given the special circumstances, they cannot be other than exercises in pure supposition. A similar

[21] Dredging Market in the United States: Results of the National Dredging Study, Symcon Publishing Co., San Pedro, California, 1976.
[22] Crown Estate Act, 1961, Section 3 (1).

contradiction arises out of the monopoly over the seabed of the outer continental shelf vested in the US Government. Licences 'for the ownership of deep-water ports' may be granted by the government at fair market rentals for the seabed and subsoil. The 'fair market rentals' are, however, determined not by the market but by the Secretary of the Interior (who, incidentally, has a corresponding power of arbitrary valuation over the 'market rental' demanded for pipeline wayleaves).[23] A Parliamentary draftsman's ink, however well directed, cannot circumvent the *de facto* power of an absolute Crown monopoly.

Many other indictments against the seabed state monopolies could be added to this citation if space permitted. We can, however, sum up, as we began, with a general observation. Where the seabed resource is vested entirely in the state, the latter cannot help entering the property market business. When on 19 January 1982, the Secretary of State for Energy moved the Second Reading of the Oil and Gas (Enterprise) Bill,[24] he reminded Parliament that the proper business of government is not the government of business. To endorse or reject his aphorism is a political choice. But there can be no doubt that the Secretary of State's viewpoint makes economic sense; the state monopoly over the seabed should be eliminated to make way for the freedom of an open market, subject always to due regard for national strategy.

Uncommon Heritage

The notion of a common heritage for all mankind in the seabed resource of the deep oceans has an engaging ring about it, especially if we allow its advocates to substitute rhetoric for reason.[25] To have any practical worth, however, an inheritance must be administered. How can mankind as a whole assume a heritage and administer it to any practical purpose? 'Mankind' is an abstract concept for which no-one has any authority or mandate to speak. If it has any meaning at all, it must embrace each and every member of the human race – all peoples and all nations. If all are to benefit, none must be left out and none must be discriminated against. Yet without a universal franchise, the democratic process cannot represent all mankind. The

---

[23] Deep Water Port Act, 1974, Section 5 (h) (3), 33 USC 1501-1524.

[24] *Hansard*, 19 January 1982, col. 169.

[25] *Cf.* R. W. Bentham, 'A Comment on the Idea of a NIEO (New International Economic Order)', paper for the International Law Association Conference, Montreal, 1982.

states which are parties to UN conferences and signatories to UN conventions are, in reality, governments – specific, national and independent. Neither individually nor in concert can they speak or act for 'mankind'. Indeed, all mankind does not accept the notion of a common heritage for itself, as we noted above (p. 38).

To set up an International Seabed Authority to administer the resources of the seabed of the deep oceans as a common heritage of all mankind is like setting up a board of directors for a company to look after the affairs of the shareholders without knowledge or record of who the shareholders are, let alone of what their wishes or best interests might be. The ISA will, therefore, embark upon life with a permanent contradiction between its commission and its competence. This contradiction is already appearing in what is proposed for its powers, policies and programmes. A common heritage should be freely and equally accessible to all 'the commoners'. Access to this common of the seabed, however, cannot be enjoyed equally by all the commoners, because only a relatively few of them have the skills and means to enable them to use the right. To make access for the strong conditional upon them helping the weak, at their own expense, is to abrogate the principle of an equal right of access to all. We cannot have it both ways.

It is contrary to the basic principles of the common law for rights in common over expendable resources to vest in an amorphous, indeterminate body of commoners.[26] It is also contrary to economic sense – hence the case for exclusive fishery zones.[27] Even if we could identify 'all mankind' and arrange for each member of the human race to be vocal in the management of the 'common heritage', the common voice and action over the seabed resource would be rendered almost ineffective by the First Law of Proprietary Magnitudes. As Dr Barry Bracewell-Milnes has written:

'This law operates most strongly under government ownership, that is, administration by officials in the nominal interest of the whole population.'[28]

If this is so with an individual nation, how much more would it be with an international sovereign authority acting in the nominal interests of all mankind?

---

[26] Cheshire, *op. cit.*, p. 294.

[27] R. N. Cooper, *An Economist's View of the Oceans*, Yale University, 1973.

[28] Barry Bracewell-Milnes, *op. cit.*, pp. 56-57 (quotation cited from p. 57).

It is no wonder, therefore, that the Law of the Sea Convention wants the ISA to require those nations with the most technical and financial capabilities to share their advantages. The preconditions for granting authority to states or companies to explore and exploit the deep-ocean beds is that advanced nations hand over skills, knowledge and finance to the developing nations. However satisfactory such a requirement may be to those who have little or no technology of their own, it is hardly conducive to the equal benefit of all mankind.[29] For how can there be equal benefits when one party is forced to make a sacrifice of skills, inventions and money to another for no or exceedingly inadequate compensation?

John Locke argued long ago[30] that those who have put skill and wealth at risk to win rewards from nature's raw material should be the possessors and owners of their winnings and discoveries. Is the modern world so changed that we should disregard this dictum of natural justice? On the other hand, the advocates of the ISA are understandably alarmed that the production of minerals from the deep-sea beds could so disrupt the world markets as to cause damage to the mineral-exporting nations – especially those in the developing world whose mineral wealth is in the land. The ISA will therefore be given powers to assess the possible consequences and to take action to prevent damage. Already, long and intricate investigations are being undertaken.[31] Their value is highly debatable. As with all national, let alone international, plans, the planners' fancy expressed in assumptions, postulates and simple guesswork is likely to be far removed from the judgements of the real world. The chance of miscalculation, however, is of relatively little moment compared with the prospect of where the ISA's powers may lead. Concern lies in the possibility that the power of the ISA, as an international institution, might be extended to cover all the inter-related mineral markets of the world.

Whichever way the ISA acts in the administration of the common heritage of mankind for the benefit of all, its inherent contradiction is likely to confound its policies and lead to ends contrary to those

---

[29] A summary of the discriminatory obligations of the ISA is given in 'The Law of the Sea Treaty: Can the US afford to sign?', in *The Backgrounder*, Heritage Foundation, Washington DC, 7 June 1982.

[30] John Locke, *Of Civil Government*, Everyman Edition, Book II, Ch. V.

[31] *Preliminary Report of the Secretary-General*, UNCLOS III, A/CONF. 62/2.84, 2 March 1982.

intended. There must be a better alternative. The fallacy of the proposal for an ISA lies in the hope of establishing an efficient collective enterprise on a world scale. The evidence of history is that coercive collectives, and the national economies based upon them, fail for want of individual reward and commitment.[32] Alternative solutions to the problems of the deep-ocean bed should, therefore (as we shall suggest in the final Section), pay more respect to the role of private property in the seabed resource. Even Rousseau and his collectivists – those radicals who built social, economic and political theories on the common will of all mankind – stoutly maintained that private property was 'le droit le plus sacré . . . dieu moral des empires'.[33]

---

[32] J. M. Buchanan's renowned comment says it all: 'Collectivised governmental attempts to do more and more have been demonstrably revealed to accomplish less and less'. (J. M. Buchanan, *The Limits of Liberty: Between Anarchy and the Leviathan*, University of Chicago Press, Chicago, 1975.)

[33] J. L. Talmon, *The Origins of Totalitarian Democracy*, Sphere Books, ed. 1970, p. 52.

VI. What Chance an Open Market?

Opposing Fixed Ideas and Inertia

The prospects for an active resource market will remain cloudy until private property in the resource is readily available for exchange. That prerequisite will in turn be governed by what the future holds for the state monopolies which still dominate today.

It has already been noted that the unconditional sovereignty which a nation exercises over its territorial waters is sufficient authority for the establishment of property rights in the seabed and its subsoil. These property rights may be public or private within the bounds of a particular national realm. The law, however, appears somewhat hesitant to draw a similar, simple relationship between the sovereign rights of nations over their respective continental shelf and property rights in the resources of the seabed. Even so, the test of pragmatism justifies our assuming that such differences as may exist lie rather in the niceties of legal theory than in practical arrangements.

Let us consider in this context how the British Parliament has handled the ownership of petroleum. Under the Petroleum (Production) Act of 1934, the property in petroleum in its natural condition was vested in the Crown (the Act uses the term 'His Majesty'). Thirty years later, the Continental Shelf Act of 1964 provided that 'any rights exercisable by the United Kingdom outside territorial waters with respect to the seabed and subsoil are vested in Her Majesty'. Further, insofar as those rights were exercisable in respect to petroleum, the provisions of the 1934 Act were to apply to the granting of licences to search and bore for and to extract it. Thus the Crown acts in exactly the same way in respect to petroleum in the continental shelf as it does as owner of petroleum in the land.

By the same token, it is reasonable to suppose that the property right of the Crown in the seabed of the territorial waters gives substance and purpose to the 'any rights' vested in the Crown over the resource of the continental shelf. In short, the Crown acts as owner of the seabed resource in both domains; and, as such, it can transfer

60

the property rights to other parties, including private ones, either absolutely or in limited tenure.

This particular thesis, based on the British model, can be applied generally to raise the question of the grounds, if any, on which nations are likely to embark upon the wholesale transfer of the ownership of the seabed resource from public to private hands, and thus to pave the way for an open resource market. There is less ambiguity in America. The statute which authorises the leasing of the outer continental shelf is entitled the 'Outer Continental Shelf *Lands* Act, 1953'. And the implication of its provisions is that, although the leases granted are for oil and gas, they are really leases of land. Section 18(a) (4) states that:

'leasing activities shall be conducted to assure receipt of fair market value for the *lands* leased and the rights conveyed by the Federal Government'.

Those who wish to nationalise all resources will rejoice in the inadvertent state ownership of the seabed resource. Whether tradition or the expediency of a novel sovereignty have done the trick is of little consequence compared with the virtual nationalisation of the seabed.[1] For the socialist, state ownership is part of political dogma. No amount of objective economic analysis will alter his conviction that public ownership facilitates central planning and bars the way to capitalistic, speculative markets in productive resources, and is therefore as essential for the seabed as for the land. Tradition can also fix ideas. In monarchies, like Britain, Norway and the Netherlands, there are traditionalists who would think it bordering on disloyalty to question the venerable royal title to the seabed. And politically-motivated ecologists, who mistrust the open-market verdict on the most efficient use of resources, tend to support state monopolies as allies in the cause of centrally-planned environments.

In most countries, the *idée fixe* is the exception. The absolute title of the Crown or state in the seabed of territorial waters, and its analogue in the continental shelf, are part of the givenness of things, accepted by the ruck of folk because no-one has seriously questioned their continuation on economic or political grounds. The inertia can be accounted for in a number of ways, the more important of which

---

[1] In the Parliamentary debate on the Continental Shelf Bill, the Opposition spokesman cynically congratulated the Conservative Minister who introduced the measure on being 'one of the greatest nationalisers'. (*Hansard*, 28 January 1964, col. 225.)

are specified in the following paragraphs, together with brief comments on their significance.

Watching the national interest

From the earliest days of the gas and oil discoveries in the North Sea and on other continental shelves, the countries which have benefitted have been concerned that their new-found wealth should not find its way into the hands of foreigners ready with cash and know-how to exploit it. Where the state holds an absolute monopoly over the supply of a resource, it can control its distribution and ensure that it is not sold off or transferred in ways harmful to the nation. Hence the repeated assurances governments of different political hues have given that maritime energy policies will accord priority to national defence and domestic economic issues.[2] To sell the seabed resource indiscriminately to the highest bidder, whoever he might be, could, on political grounds, appear not to be in the national interest.

Concern is understandable but not necessarily justified. The market we are adumbrating is a market in the seabed resource, not one dealing exclusively in hydrocarbon deposits, which is only one element of the total seabed resource. Furthermore, in the UK, France and other countries where property rights in petroleum were nationalised long before it was discovered in the seabed, it would be possible to offer indiscriminatory interests in the seabed resource, as with estates in the land, while leaving the title to petroleum and other nationalised minerals where it is, in the hands of the state. By so doing, fears that the nation's newly-acquired wealth would be sold off could be allayed.

While the prior nationalisation of minerals could have been a contributory factor, however, it would be a mistake to see it as a crucial event leading to the state and Crown titles in the seabed. These monopolies exist in countries like the USA where minerals under private land are private property. They also apply to the seabed resource as a whole and not exclusively to selected, nationalised mineral rights. What is more, it is questionable whether the nationalisation of landward petroleum, gas and minerals should be extended

---

[2] On moving the Second Reading of the Oil and Gas (Enterprise) Bill in the House of Commons, for example, the then Secretary of State for Energy said: 'Our vital strategic and other national interests are fully safeguarded by the complex statutory framework of regulatory controls, participation agreements and taxation, all of which remain, and will remain, fully in force.' (*Hansard*, 19 January 1982, col. 169.)

without demur to the seabed oil pools and coal seams. In Britain, the nationalisers won the day in the 1930s because the proprietary patterns of the surface lands did not coincide with nature's coal deposits and oil fields.[3] The state monopoly owners could dispose of estates in the seabed resource, however, to accord with the coincidence and whereabouts (roughly determined) of mineral strata and oil pools.[4]

As for national defence, there may be apprehension that an open market in the seabed resource would admit into national territory undesirable foreigners who, while professing to pursue genuine commercial aims, harboured nefarious designs against the vendor nation. But numerous countries prohibit the sale of interests in *land* to aliens. Similar restraints could be imposed over private transactions in the seabed resource market. Moreover, the original state conveyances could reserve a right to inspect operations and a power to invalidate the titles of offenders.[5]

Neither navigation in the high seas nor the right to fish need be affected by changes in the ownership of the seabed. Control of navigation could, as at present, lie with the Admiralty, the harbour boards and other nautical authorities; and control of fishing activities could also remain where it is. The possibility of discrete activities in the maritime realm was well described by Sir Cecil Hurst, an internationally recognised authority on maritime law and legal adviser to the Foreign Office, 60 years ago:

'The claim to the exclusive ownership of a portion of the bed of the sea and to the wealth which it produces . . . is not inconsistent with the universal right of navigation in the open sea or with the common right of the public to fish in the high seas.'[6]

---

[3] House of Lords debate on the Petroleum (Production) Bill, *Hansard*, 19 April 1934, cols. 661-694; House of Commons debate on the Coal Bill, *Hansard*, 22 November 1937, cols. 871-990.

[4] A cogent argument has recently been advanced by Michael Beesley and Stephen Littlechild for a policy to sell off the state-owned coal pits of Britain to private owners. (*Lloyds Bank Review*, July 1983.)

[5] When, in the 1970s, the USA was much concerned with domestic and other energy supplies, special obligations were imposed upon the Federal Energy Administration to conduct a comprehensive review of the foreign ownership of resources, to monitor all changes, and to report to the Congress on the extent of such ownership and its influence upon domestic energy sources and supplies. (Federal Energy Administration Act, 1974, 15 USC, 761-790h, Section 26.)

[6] Sir Cecil J. B. Hurst, 'Whose is the Bed of the Sea?', *British Yearbook of International Law*, Vol. IV, 1923/24, pp. 34-43.

Pathways of reform

Failure to act towards the seabed resource in the same way as towards
the land has meant that each of the several elements of which the
resource is composed – hydrocarbons, minerals, natural produce,
latent energy, dumping grounds, installation sites, fisheries, and so on
– has been treated as a resource in isolation. Piecemeal exploitation
has followed. In many countries, notably Britain, there has been an
obvious lack of co-ordinated policy on resource development. What
is required is a more acute sense of ownership of the seabed as a whole.

To own something absolutely gives the owner the greatest power
over its use. A landowner is in the best position to co-ordinate the
uses of his land and to do so to a purpose. His co-ordinating control
extends to the boundaries of his estate – his proprietary unit. That unit
can be too extensive to be efficiently managed, as is commonly the
case where the state is the supreme owner and all the land resources
of a nation are in one public proprietary unit.[7] Successful co-ordina-
tion and efficient management are dependant on the pattern of ownership. Hence the virtue of distributing land resources into manageable
units and, particularly, into private ownership. The beneficial power
of ownership can be limited, but not entirely nullified, by public
control of uses.

What is here true of the land is true also of the seabed. Estates in
the seabed resource, on all fours with the fee simple[8] of English land
law, could – as in land – be subjected to a system of public control
over resource use. An attempt to anticipate something along these lines
was made in March 1983 when a private member's Bill[9] was introduced into Parliament to extend the land-use planning system over
the seabed of all internal waters, the territorial sea and the continental
shelf. The seabed resource could thus have a régime which in its
ownership, marketing and control was similar to its counterpart on
the land.

To offer to private buyers near-absolute ownership of interests in
the seabed might be premature with an unprepared public opinion.
Something approximating the benefits of such a market, however,

---

[7] The First Law of Proprietary Magnitudes operates (above, p. 57).

[8] A 'fee simple' in English land law describes an unconditional inheritance. For a fuller
definition of the legal term 'fee simple', Cheshire, *op. cit.*, p. 109.

[9] The Crown Estate (Foreshore and Seabed) (Amendment) Bill, 22 April 1983.

could be attained step-by-step, by replacing licences with long-term leases, offered for premiums and freely alienable. Alternatively, a system of tenure on the lines of the Scottish feu system would provide proprietary control over the use of the seabed, exercised by the state over private marketable property.[10] The Crown or state would hold a superior estate, the *dominium directum*; and the lesser estate, the *dominium utile*, would be the merchandise on the open property market. Under such a system, dredging companies, for example, would compete among themselves and with other buyers in the open market for the *dominium utile* over areas of the seabed they wished to acquire. The interest purchased would be subject to restrictions safeguarding navigation, conservation, and so on, imposed under covenant with the state as the holder of the superior interest. The result would be a free market in the inferior interests which would be held privately and be subject to the proprietary control of covenants administered by the state – a control which could be eased or intensified as policy required.

Another path of reform would be to introduce a zonal approach to denationalisation of the seabed resource. The introduction of private property and an open property market could be limited temporarily to the seabed of the territorial sea or, as in Holland, to the near approaches. Alternatively, areas could be far narrower and confined to harbours, marina sites, sedentary fishing grounds, places with non-metallic mineral deposits, and so on, where evidence existed of a definite but suppressed market demand. However designed, policies for an open-market régime in the seabed would depend in most countries on the state or Crown authorities abandoning their negative posture for a more positive approach to marketing and development.

Getting Out of the Rut

It cannot be over-emphasised that the pursuit of our theme of a market in the seabed resource is an excursion into the unknown. Nothing is going to happen unless the monopolies now in possession are willing to relax their hold and establish an open market. We have briefly examined how this might be brought about and the problems which would attend the change; that is to say, we have examined the implica-

---

[10] A similar proprietary control of land use is to be found in Malaysia under the Malaysian Land Code.

tions from the supply side. But, even if governments were prepared to move towards more open markets, the question remains: What would be the likely response from the buying side? Would those now holding licences and other interests want to be the owners of more substantial property rights with the power to market them? And would there be a general interest in the investment potential of property development on the seabed?

Costs of acquisition

The answers cannot be other than speculative. For one thing, attitudes to buying could be influenced by the costs of acquisition when the first offers were made by the state. Clearly, for a licensee to take a freehold interest would involve an exchange transaction requiring a monetary consideration in addition to the surrendered licence in most cases. The value of what was given up would be a measure of the cost of acquisition. No-one could forecast what the cost would be with any degree of precision; it would depend, among other things, on the timing of the offer of an alternative. It would also depend on the conditions of choice granted in the first place.

Even if the state, as supreme owner of the seabed, decided to offer freeholds in the resource, some arbitrary decisions would have to be made about the sites being offered and how and when to place them on the market. Such decisions by the state as monopoly supplier would not be made in response to a demonstrated market demand, because until the decisions were made the market would not know what was available to bid for. As primary moves away from monopoly towards an open market, the decisions would be in the nature of arbitrarily planned initiatives. Upon these decisions, however, would turn the nature of the choice to be made by the private purchaser; and upon the nature of the choice would rest the ultimate cost to be borne. With the state as supreme owner of the seabed resource, there has been hitherto no opportunity of choosing and, therefore, no past evidence of what the response to a right to choose might have been. Before we could speculate on what the response might be, we would have to know what the state intended to offer. The running would therefore be with the state as monopoly owner. If a genuine policy of disposal were pursued, supplies would have to be made as flexible and responsive to demand as possible. The true answer to the question of cost would not be known until the market was operating, for only the opportunity to choose in an open market can give expression to that subjective judgement on which true cost ultimately depends.[11] For the time being, we can proceed only by way of conjecture.

With the exception of brokerage charges, acquiring freeholds or absolute interests in the seabed need incur transaction costs no higher than those under the present system; the former could even be cheaper. Operators in Britain, whatever their objectives may be – oil extraction, mineral dredging, shellfish culture – have in any event to bear the expense of initial surveys to find what they are looking for. They must then make applications for rights to explore further and to exploit. As holder of the supreme title to the seabed resource, the state registers the interests granted; and the parties to transactions bear their own legal costs. All that is required for an open market in freeholds, or the equivalent, is the conversion of current limited interests into unlimited ones – a matter merely of legal wording. New interests would be identified, in the first instance, either by the state when offering them to the market, or by would-be purchasers approaching the state vendor with propositions.

Identifying the boundaries of holdings on the seabed and policing them against trespassers are other sources of transaction costs. These, however, are not peculiar to private freeholds or absolute interests. Such costs are equally substantial under the present system of derivative titles to leases and licences. It would be almost essential to have a Land Titles Register to provide a public record and to secure private freeholds in the seabed resource. There are instances in Britain where non-Crown titles to the seabed are already registered in the Public Land Registry – for example, the holdings of the Medway Ports Authority in the tidal reaches of the Medway and Swale. Long leases of and licences in the seabed are usually and for efficiency registered by the grantors. Ideally, registration as practised under the present system would continue with modifications in an open resource market. Evidence from dealings in limited interests does not suggest, therefore, that a change to an open market in unlimited interests would be likely to create or be hampered by the emergence of additional costs. Once the market was functioning properly, it would operate like any other property market. The property market in land

---

[11] J. M. Buchanan, 'Cost Theory in Retrospect', Introduction to LSE *Essays on Cost*, ed. J. M. Buchanan and G. F. Tilley, London School of Economics, 1973, pp. 14 and 15.

would not survive if its transaction costs were too high. The same would be true of a market in the seabed resource.

Brokerage costs

An open market would doubtless be operated by qualified brokerage firms engaged in the present property market. Brokerage costs are unknown where derivative property interests are granted by an absolute state authority in response to requests. Brokerage can be regarded as the cost of acquiring the benefits of an open market, in all types of estate and proprietary interest, with its flexibility, benefits of distribution and relative freedom from direct state control. Brokerage is tantamount to resource owners passing a fraction of their capitalised rent to the brokerage profession in consideration for services rendered – a distribution of wealth into wider employment.

Benefits of experience

People who have spent all their lives in a centrally-planned economy often find the freedom of unfettered thought and action bewildering; they become used to their fetters. The longer the seabed monopolies and their ways remain, the more difficult it will be for those accustomed to government control to imagine a change to a freer way. Not infrequently, oil companies have admitted to a preference for the exercise of government discretion in the allocation of production licences rather than having to chance their arm in the competitive arena of bids and tenders. In contrast, where established procedures display something of the freedom of the market – as with the 'auctioning' of oil production leases in the USA – buyers accustomed to the dictates of governments in other countries become active bidders and, not exceptionally, among the successful.[12]

Experience of an open market in the seabed resource could be self-advancing. In Britain today, for example, a dredging company seeking new areas for its operations has to apply for a licence to the Crown Estate Commissioners and then to face the prospect of prolonged inter-departmental cross-inquiries. In a fully functioning open market, such a company would go shopping for its resource needs aided only

---

[12] For instance, at the Federal Government's auction of oil and gas leases in the Beaufort Sea in October 1982, BP (and its American subsidiary Sohio) outbid all other competitors for 25 exploration leases with a bid of £373 million.

by self-appointed agents. The way in which the market offered its holdings would, in time, come to reflect the pattern of demand. Marginal prices would set boundaries to resource-use patterns and ownership units. The arbitrary judgements of today's ways would give place to a system where supplies more exactly satisfied demands – an improvement which could but stimulate demand and hence add to market experience. The general investor would learn how to satisfy particular operators. And the purchasers of extensive estates, such as oil companies buying up seabed resources for initial exploration work, would learn the art of marketing lesser interests to satisfy multi-resource demands – or, with the onset of profitable oil flows, they would make specific lease-back arrangements to the benefit of general investors (the buyer-lessors) and themselves.

Planning control

Buyers in a market for the seabed resource would think of themselves as landowners do, not as entrepreneurs licensed to dredge, mine or fish. What would have been acquired would be a right of ownership in the seabed resource, irrespective of the uses of the resource. A government which wanted to impose public control over private uses of the seabed would be able to do so by controlling the power of the landowner. It would be a direct and single line of control. Such relative simplicity as a market in the seabed resource would introduce ought to streamline bureaucratic processes, ease costs, save development time and generally act to commend a free market. It would, moreover, be wholly in keeping with the notion of planning controls over land use being extended to cover the use and development of the seabed resource. The simpler world of private property and its resource market would remove or ease the conflicts which can arise under current conditions where operators in the seabed have to have wayleaves, servitudes and similar ancillary rights to accommodate their licensed operations. A private estate in the seabed would have its own easements and incorporeal hereditaments appurtenant to it to serve the legitimate interests of the owner – as happens with estates in the land.

Removing a basic confusion

If he is a competent manager, the owner of a land estate which has mines and quarries among its farms and forests will have no difficulty in distinguishing his capital investment in the land and buildings from the capital in the estate enterprises, with its fixed and moveable plant provided by the entrepreneurs, quarrymasters and mining companies who hold leases from him. He would dispose of the estate on the property market for a price which reflected the market value (and hence the yield) of the land capital. When, as sometimes happens, mineral rights are excluded from a sale of an estate in the land, the vendor retains a corporeal interest in the mineral-bearing land from which he receives royalties and rent. Minerals are not sold as chattels or commodities away from the land.

This same outlook is required for the seabed. The important distinction between resource capital and fixed and moveable working capital has been blurred in seabed régimes because of the practice of disposing of the resource elements (oil, gas, minerals, and so on) as chattels apart from the seabed resource which embodies them. The upshot has been for oil and mineral companies in particular to make no distinction between the assets which give them rights in the seabed (licences and leases) and the products extracted from it. The confusion is an unhealthy aspect of capital investment in seabed development. And it is largely responsible for the failure to distinguish between enterprise income and rent, as also for the practice in Britain and elsewhere of virtually taxing rent from the seabed as if it were oil revenue. A property market buying and selling estates in the seabed resource upon which various production enterprises depended would prevent such confusion and would ensure that each production factor, resource capital and enterprise capital, earned its own reward. Removing the confusion in this way would be essential before capital from the property development companies now operating on land could be attracted to the development of the seabed.

All countries with mixed economies where the government is set on realising the potential of the seabed will, sooner or later, have to accept and encourage private property and a resource market as the efficient tools for shaping the economy of the seabed to fit into and harmonise with the land-based economic structure. A state could develop the seabed resource itself through nationalised production and development companies. But this could push the combined economies of land and seabed resources far towards a centralised régime. To balance the mix, the private company should be entitled and encouraged to play its part, and should be free to invest how and where it judged it expedient. To have to operate within the onerous confines and conditions of derivative and narrowly-drawn licences or similar devices granted by a state monopoly can be economically damaging – as, for example, where a state landlord imposes conditions in leases which frustrate lessees in providing the necessary capital to maximise returns both to itself and to the land.

How much better it would be for the oil companies to operate free of the niggling sanctions which, in many places, control even the initial survey and exploration! As the owner of a freehold or similar interest in the seabed resource, a firm should be free, within very general limits, to initiate and pursue all reasonable development activities. If it struck oil, a licence might be essential to exploit the find – as was the practice with coal in Britain before the coal rights were nationalised. Licences were used to prevent conflict where surface interests were not identical with the underground coal deposits. For the reasons already discussed,[13] however, a resource market in the seabed might be free of these and similar controls which were imposed to meet conditions on land.

Mutual Bonds of Freedom

The case for the freedom of the seabed and an open market in the seabed resource is no less cogent for the deep abyss beyond the national continental shelf than it is for the seabed of coastal waters. The arguments are the same but stronger.

The transcendental affirmation that the deep seabed is the common heritage of mankind, although beyond the hope of expression in practical administration, could find fulfilment in a notional common sovereignty. Given the right administration, a common sovereignty could be the source of private property in the deep-ocean *fundus* and of a seabed resource market.[14]

Give and take in the deep ocean

Whatever else the ISA, its Assembly and its other organs might come

---

[13] Above, pp. 62–63.

[14] One of the reasons why the British Government declined to sign the Law of the Sea Convention of 10 December 1982 was that certain provisions 'seek to make new law which would give obligatory effect for the participants in the Convention to the idea of the common heritage of mankind set out in General Assembly Resolutions . . .'. (Statement by Ambassador J. E. Powell-Jones at UNCLOS, Montego Bay, 8 December 1982.)

to stand for, they could not symbolise the common heritage of mankind. The Authority, as sole planner and administrator of the seabed resource, would exclude from the so-called 'common heritage' all nationals and peoples who did not conform to its policies and sanctions. It therefore has all the makings of state government replete with powers of both *imperium* and *dominium*. One of its first jobs would be to 'advise' nations of the boundaries between their respective sovereignties and its own imperial realm.

Ideally, the ISA would be there to administer the deep seabed on behalf of the nations of the world. Some nations, however, have centrally-planned economies while others value open markets and free enterprise. The point was made earlier (pp. 70-71) that, in a mixed economy, stresses can arise between the state landlord and private lessees which are harmful to economic development. The ISA would, in effect, face a world mixed economy. For it to administer the deep-ocean resources vested in it as if it were holding the nationalised lands of a centrally-planned economy could precipitate similar stresses and strains – so serious, perhaps, as to undermine its strength and impair its competence. Its success would depend on the continuing willingness of nations with capital and skills to seek leases in the seabed. If its 'collective' purpose required leasing covenants which were unacceptable to the private enterprise lessees, the leases would not be taken up and the ISA would not be able to operate effectively.

The Law of the Sea Convention is now open for signature, but its provisions will not be binding on signatories until one year after 60 nations have *ratified* it. The USA had earlier declared its intention not to sign, and the non-signatories also include, at present, the UK and various other countries, not all of which are Western. Only time will show which countries, if any, line up behind the US lead. Signing the Convention can, at this stage, be conditional on the acceptability of the small print of rules and regulations which ultimately emerges from the Preparatory Commission. With the fairest of winds in its favour, it would still be some years before the ISA became fully operative.

In the meantime, irrespective of the international régime and the prospect of licensing control by the ISA, those who know best are becoming deeply sceptical of the long-term industrial and commercial value of deep-sea mining – as a consequence of re-assessing the mineral potential of the deep-seabed nodules and the cost of mining them.

An Alternative International Arrangement

These uncertainties, and the prospect of difficulties and perhaps failure if the ISA adopts too *dirigiste* a line, have stimulated thinking about alternatives. Since the summer of 1982, a few Western countries have proposed a Reciprocating States Agreement (RSA)[15] which has now become little more than an understanding among the participating countries to prevent the overlap of claims. The aim is to harmonise the municipal legislation of the individual states which are parties to the agreement in order to achieve mutual recognition of claims under international law to the deep-ocean bed. Something along these lines will be necessary even if the ISA *is* set up; for the pioneer states (those which have laid claim to mining sites on the basis of investments already made) will have to provide the ISA with evidence of agreed methods of recognition and operation.[16]

The RSA could, however, serve a double purpose. In the long term it could be an alternative for nations to turn to should the ISA fail to become a fully representative world body. Mutual understanding along these lines is preferable to a world authority controlling the seabed industrial activities of companies and nations. Moreover, it would be much more amenable to the idea of private property and an international market in the seabed resource.

A Common Heritage to Private Property

However, as we approach the end of this *Hobart Paperback*, let us stay with the problems of the ISA. It was suggested above that the theory of a common heritage of mankind in the deep seabed could find expression in a real but notional sovereignty vested in a body like the ISA. The ISA could rule over the seabed much as a state government rules over its lands to recognise and protect private property in them. No nation or people should be barred from participating in the common heritage; all nations should have a right of access. But those who by dint of forethought, courage, ability, and command of

---

[15] Treaty Series No. 46 (1982): *Agreement concerning Interim Arrangements relating to Polymetallic Nodules of the Deep Sea Bed*, Washington DC, 2 September 1982; Cmnd. 8685, HMSO, October 1982.

[16] The Preparatory Commission has already run into trouble because the USSR has indicated the co-ordinates of the areas it claims as a pioneer investor and has asked for an exchange of co-ordinates by other claimants by 1 May 1983, or the formal registration of its own claim. (LOS/PCN/4, 8 April 1983.)

resources could win their way to find and open mining sites or execute other activities of a commercial nature, should be able to look to the ISA for recognition and formal registration of their just claims to property rights. In consideration of recognition and registration, the ISA could raise levies from registered claimants. Income from the levies would augment the general funds supplied through the United Nations to support the ISA.

In addition to its property registration service, the Authority could and should act as a world agency. As an honest broker, it would bring together developing nations and those with the knowledge and means to help them. At the same time, it would assist with negotiations and the forging of joint ventures in operations and joint tenancies in ownership. These simply stated ideas would obviously require a revised convention. The effort would certainly be worthwhile if it resulted in an abiding freedom for the world's seabed in harmony with the notion of a common heritage of mankind.

VII. Conclusions

This *Hobart Paperback* has drawn attention to a kind of accident whose consequences for all nations could, if not recognised and checked, exert a profound influence upon future economic developments and freedoms which are dependent upon private property and markets in natural resources.

The land mass which lies submerged under the marginal seas of nations and beneath the deep oceans where national claims are neutral has, within the space of a few years, become a realm rich in realisable resources and development potential. Both outside and within the provisions of UN treaties and conventions, nations have extended the boundaries of their national jurisdictions to lay claim to new and extensive sovereignties over the seabed resource. The very process of national assertion – of staking out claims to the seabed – has inadvertently established state ownership over the submerged land mass, the seabed and its subsoil.

The simplicity of truth is so often obscured, and the nationalised seabeds are a good example. This *Hobart Paperback* has attempted to make the simple truth plain and to ask how long the consequences of this accident of history are to go unchecked. Merely to recognise that, in a country like Britain, two-thirds of the nation's natural resources of land and sea are nationalised, more as a result of accident than political design, is a step forward. It is, however, a wasted effort if we do not go further and inquire about the future prospects for free markets in the seabed resource taking over from the state monopolies.

What seems to be an unthinking acceptance of the monopoly of the state over the disposition of the seabed resource has, among its more regrettable consequences, provided a pattern for the future administration of the seabed resource of the deep oceans. The idea that ownership of the seabed resource must inevitably entail *state* ownership has led UNCLOS III to conceive an international authority for the seabed which would act virtually as a sovereign state, to own and administer the seabed resources of the deep oceans. Nationalisation of the seabed by default has thus prompted the deliberate internationalisation of what are today freely accessible resources.

This *Hobart Paperback* has argued that the time has now come to face up to the consequences of the nationalisation of the seabed, to recognise what has happened and is happening, and to put a stop to it by allowing scope for private property and an open resource market. Because such nationalisation is more accidental than deliberate, there is little or no *political* prejudice to overcome even though an uninformed and sentimental public opinion may need to be educated and pointed in the right direction. Internationally, it is a different matter. The proposals for an International Seabed Authority are not accidental but designed to a political end. Yet that in no way justifies them – rather the reverse. We have shown that a common heritage of mankind in the resources of the deep oceans need not, in principle, preclude private property and a market in the seabed resource.

Economically, there is a near-unanswerable case against the Western nations preserving their national state monopolies over the seabed. Private property is the bastion of individual liberties; and an open market is an essential condition for a sound policy towards the distribution of the seabed resource. For many countries, notably Britain, a state monopoly over so large a proportion of national assets as the developed seabed will occupy will produce a serious imbalance in their mixed economies.

Once government has made up its mind to demolish the seabed monopolies, the process could be phased in gradually. There would, for example, be less legal quibbling about selling interests in the seabed of the territorial waters of Britain than with disposing of similar interests in the continental shelf. To the present British Government, which is looking for ways to reduce public borrowing and cut taxation, a disposal policy for the seabed resource should make good sense.

Further Reading

Books: (Topics)

Barston, R. P., and Birnie, Patricia (eds.), *The Maritime Dimension*, George Allen & Unwin, London, 1980.

Brown, E. D., *The Legal Regime of Hydrospace*, The Library of World Affairs Number 70, Stevens & Sons, London, 1971.

Clarke, Robin, *More than enough? An optimistic assessment of world energy*, The Unesco Press, 1982.

Dunning, F. W., *Geophysical Exploration*, Natural Environment Research Council, Institute of Geological Sciences, The Geological Museum, HMSO, London, 1970.

Dam, Kenneth W., *Oil Resources: Who gets What How?*, University of Chicago Press, Chicago and London, 1976.

Fawcett, J. E. S., and Parry, Audrey, *Law and International Resource Conflicts*, Royal Institute of International Affairs, Clarendon Press, Oxford, 1981.

Marston, Geoffrey, *The Marginal Seabed: United Kingdom Legal Practice*, Clarendon Press, Oxford, 1981.

Sibthorp, M. M. (ed.), *The North Sea Challenge and Opportunity*, The David Davies Memorial Institute of International Studies, Europa Publications, London, 1975.

Sibthorp, M. M. (ed.), *Oceanic Management Conflicting Uses of the Celtic Sea and other Western UK Waters*, The David Davies Memorial Institute of International Studies, Europa Publications, London, 1977.

UN Ocean Economics and Technology Office, *Manganese Nodules: Dimensions and Perspectives*, D. Reidel Publishing Co., Dordrecht, Holland, 1979.

UN Ocean Economics and Technology Branch, *Assessment of Manganese Nodule Resources: The Data and the Methodologies*, Seabed Minerals Series Vol. I., Graham & Trotman, London, 1982.

Christy, F. T., and Scott, A., *The Common Wealth in Ocean Fisheries; Some Problems of Growth and Economic Allocation*, The Johns Hopkins Press, Baltimore and London, 1972.

McDougal, M. S., and Burke, W. T., *The Public Order of the Oceans*, Yale University Press, New Haven and London, 1962.

Oxman, Bernard H., Caron, David D., and Buderi, Charles L. (eds.), *The Law of the Sea: US Policy Dilemma*, The Institute for Contemporary Studies, San Francisco, 1983.

Books: (General Background)

Akehurst, Michael, *A Modern Introduction to International Law* (4th Edn.), George Allen & Unwin, London, 1982.

Denman, D. R., *The Place of Property: A New Recognition of the Functions and Form of Property Rights in Land*, Geographical Publications Ltd., Berkhamsted, 1978.

Denman, D. R., and Prodano, Sylvio, *Land Use: An Introduction to Proprietary Land Use Analysis*, George Allen & Unwin, London, 1972.

Booklets, Memoranda and Articles:

Backgrounder, *The Law of the Sea Treaty: Can the US Afford to Sign?*, A United Nations Assessment Project Study, The Heritage Foundation, Washington DC, June 1982.

Bentham, R. W., 'The Third UN Law of the Sea Conference: the final stage', *The International Contract, Law & Finance Review*, Vol. 2, No. 2, March 1981.

Cheung, S., 'The Structure of a Contract and the Theory of a Non-Exclusive Resource', as appearing in Furubotn, E. G., and Pejovich, S. (eds.), *The Economics of Property Rights*, Ballinger Publishing Co., Cambridge, Mass., 1974.

Christy, Francis T., 'Property Rights in the World Ocean', *Natural Resources Journal*, School of Law, University of New Mexico, New Mexico.

Cooper, Richard N., 'An Economist's View of the Oceans', *Journal of World Trade Law*, July-August 1975.

Gibson, John, 'The Ownership of the Seabed under British Territorial Waters', *Journal of David Davies Memorial Institute*, Vol. VI, No. 2, November 1978.

UN Office Geneva, *Convention of Law of Sea Adopted*, Press Release SEA/154, 30 April 1982.

UN New York, *Convention on the Law of the Sea, Working Paper 1*, as prepared for Drafting Committee, 7 June 1982.

UN UK Information Centre, *Nine-year UN Conference of Law of Sea Ends*, Ref. BR/82/42, 31 December 1982.

Webley, Simon, *The Law of the Sea Treaty: Some Crucial Questions for the UK*, Institute for European Defence & Strategic Studies, London, 1982.

Questions for Discussion

1. To what extent is the analogy between the seabed resource and the land mass sustainable?

2. If the analogy is sound, does it follow that there should be open markets in interests in the seabed resource similar to land or property markets?

3. How have the present universal state monopolies over the coastal seabed resource come about?

4. To what extent do the present and the foreseeable uses of the seabed resource complement or conflict with each other?

5. Is the notion that the seabed resource of the deep oceans is the common heritage of mankind no more than an idealistic platitude, or can it be given practical expression?

6. In what ways have the present state monopolies over the coastal seabed resource led to economic inefficiencies in its use and distribution?

7. If private absolute ownership of interests in the seabed resource were to be established, to what extent, if any, would there be a case for public control of the use of the resource?

8. What distinction do you draw between a tax on the revenue from the seabed resource and economic rent?

9. What practical policies would have to be followed in the UK to establish private property and a free market in the seabed resource of (a) the territorial sea and (b) the continental shelf?

10. 'Full property rights over the seabed resource should be vested in those who first identify its wealth and successfully exploit it.' Would the adoption of such a principle lead to anarchy in the ocean or to efficient and just national and international development policies?

Markets under the Sea?

D. R. DENMAN

1. The ownership and marketing of the seabed are of major economic and social consequence now that scientific knowledge has made possible the exploitation of the seabed.

2. Products from the seabed—oil, minerals, shellfish—have their own markets which are distinguishable from a market in the seabed resource itself, even though they have an important influence upon it.

3. There are growing demands for access to the seabed arising from the claims of governments, industrial and commercial enterprises, and advances in technology.

4. Governments of coastal states have established sovereign rights over the seabed which have led to state ownership and monopoly.

5. The Law of the Sea Convention envisages the creation of an international authority with exclusive powers to grant access to the resources of the deep oceans as the common heritage of mankind—in other words, an international public monopoly which can only slow down development.

6. Users of the seabed today are wholly dependent on grants of limited interests in it from the state monopolies.

7. Full private property rights and a free market in the seabed are the preconditions for it it be used and developed in the most economically efficient manner.

8. The state monopolies inhibit flexible investment, prevent a full recognition of the potential for rent, encourage inertia, and impose excessive charges on the use of resources.

9. The prospects for a market in the seabed resource depend upon a consideration of the national interest, the attitudes of potential buyers, and the outcome of experiments in adjusting supplies to meet unknown demands.

10. Private property in the seabed resource of the deep oceans is a feasible and desirable objective, and is compatible with the ideal of a common heritage of mankind.

Hobart Paperback 17 is published (price £2·50) by

THE INSTITUTE OF ECONOMIC AFFAIRS
2 Lord North Street, Westminster
London SW1P 3LB   Telephone: 01-799 3745

IEA PUBLICATIONS

Subscription Service

An annual subscription is the most convenient way to obtain our publications. Every title we produce in all our regular series will be sent to you immediately on publication and without further charge, representing a substantial saving.

Subscription rates

Britain: £15.00 p.a. including postage.

£14.00 p.a. if paid by Banker's Order.

£10.00 p.a. teachers and students who pay *personally*.

Europe and South America: £20 or equivalent.

Other countries: Rates on application. In most countries subscriptions are handled by local agents.

*These rates are *not* available to companies or to institutions.

To: The Treasurer, Institute of Economic Affairs,

2 Lord North Street,

Westminster, London SW1P 3LB.

I should like to subscribe beginning ....

I enclose a cheque/postal order for:

☐ £15.00

☐ Please send me a Banker's Order form

☐ Please send me an Invoice

☐ £10.00 [I am a teacher/student at...................................]

Name ....

Address ....

....

Signed .... Date ....

HPB17